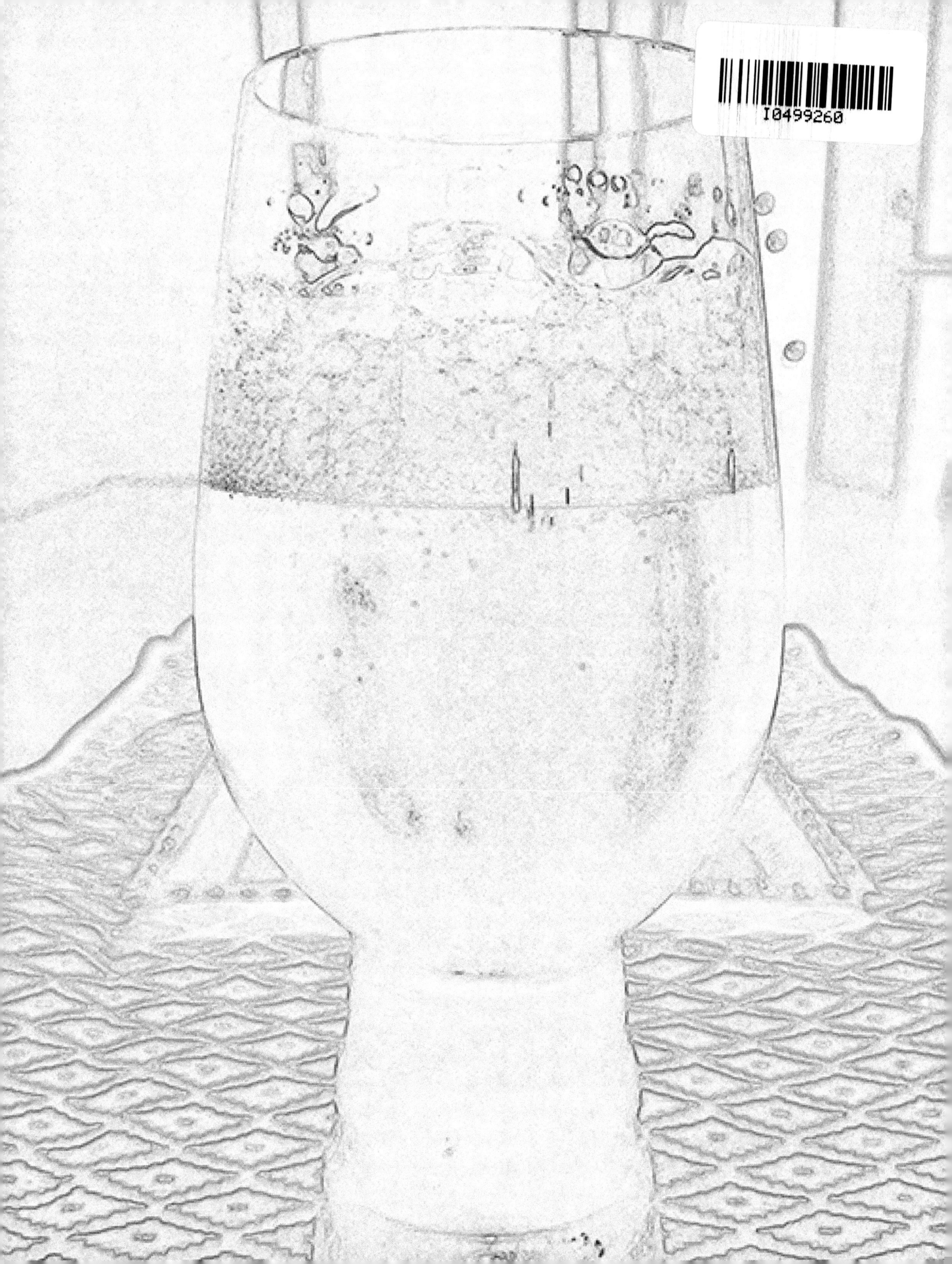

MAKE
YOUR
OWN
BEER
CAN

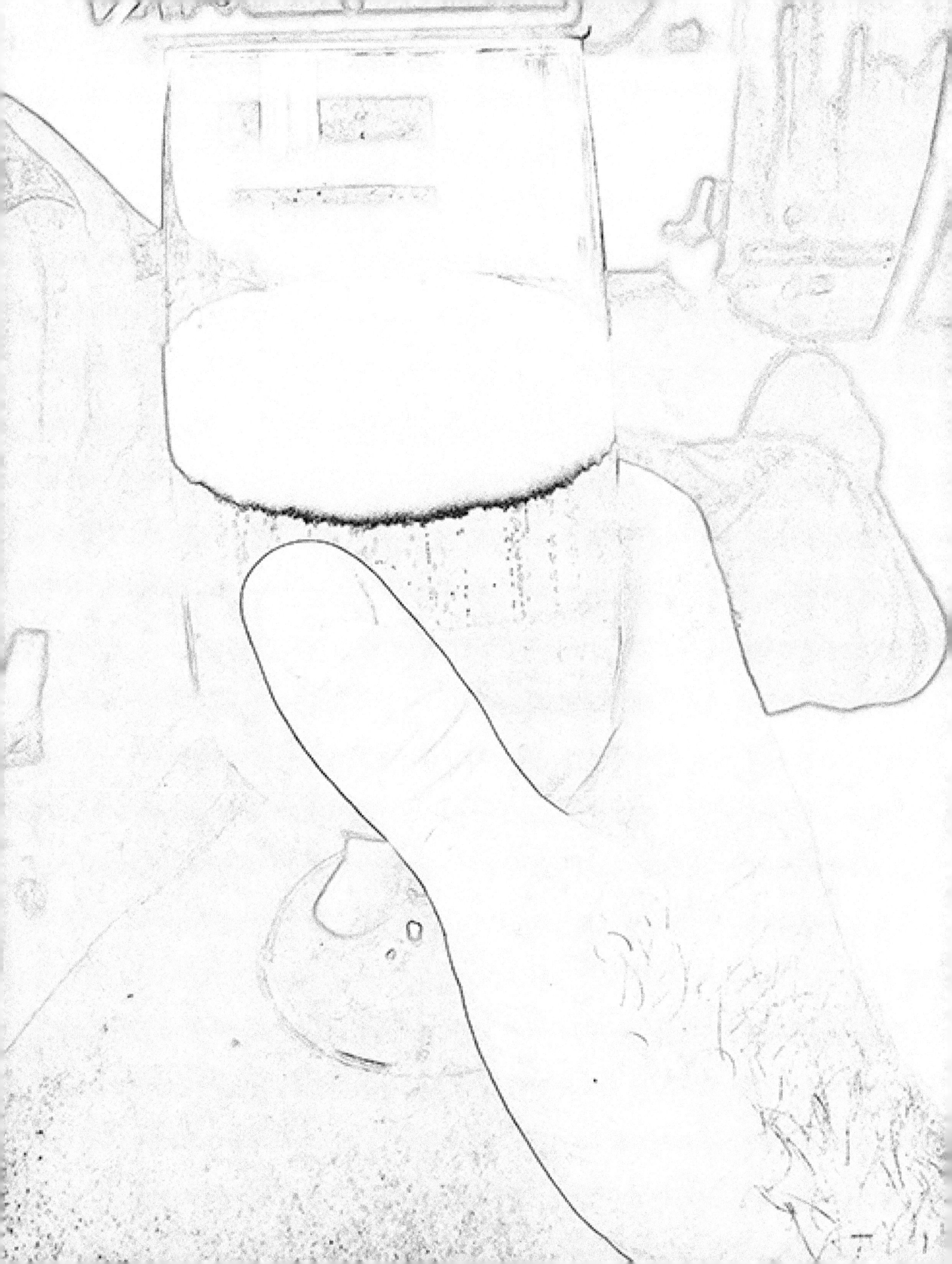

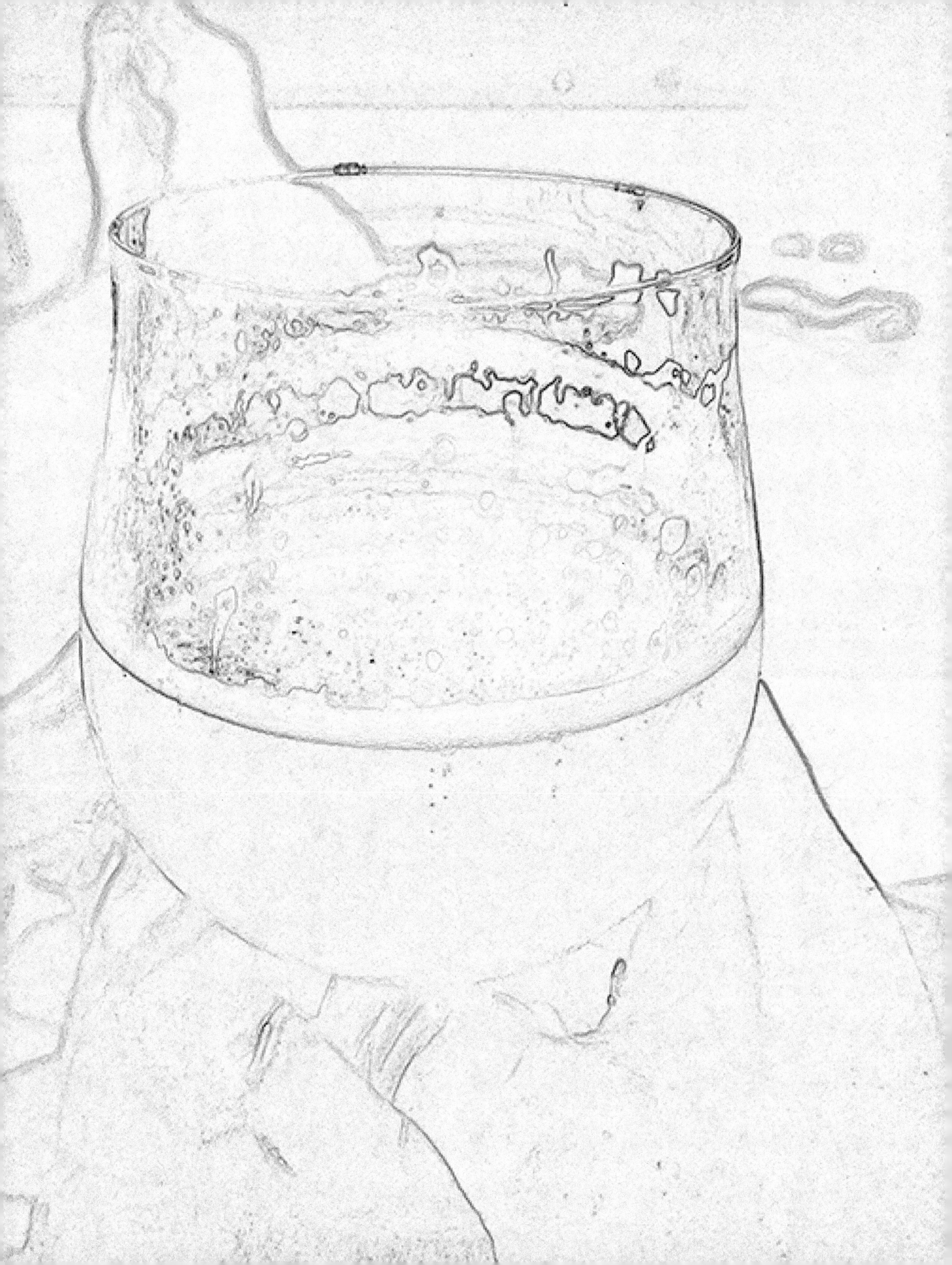

MAKE YOUR OWN BEER LABEL

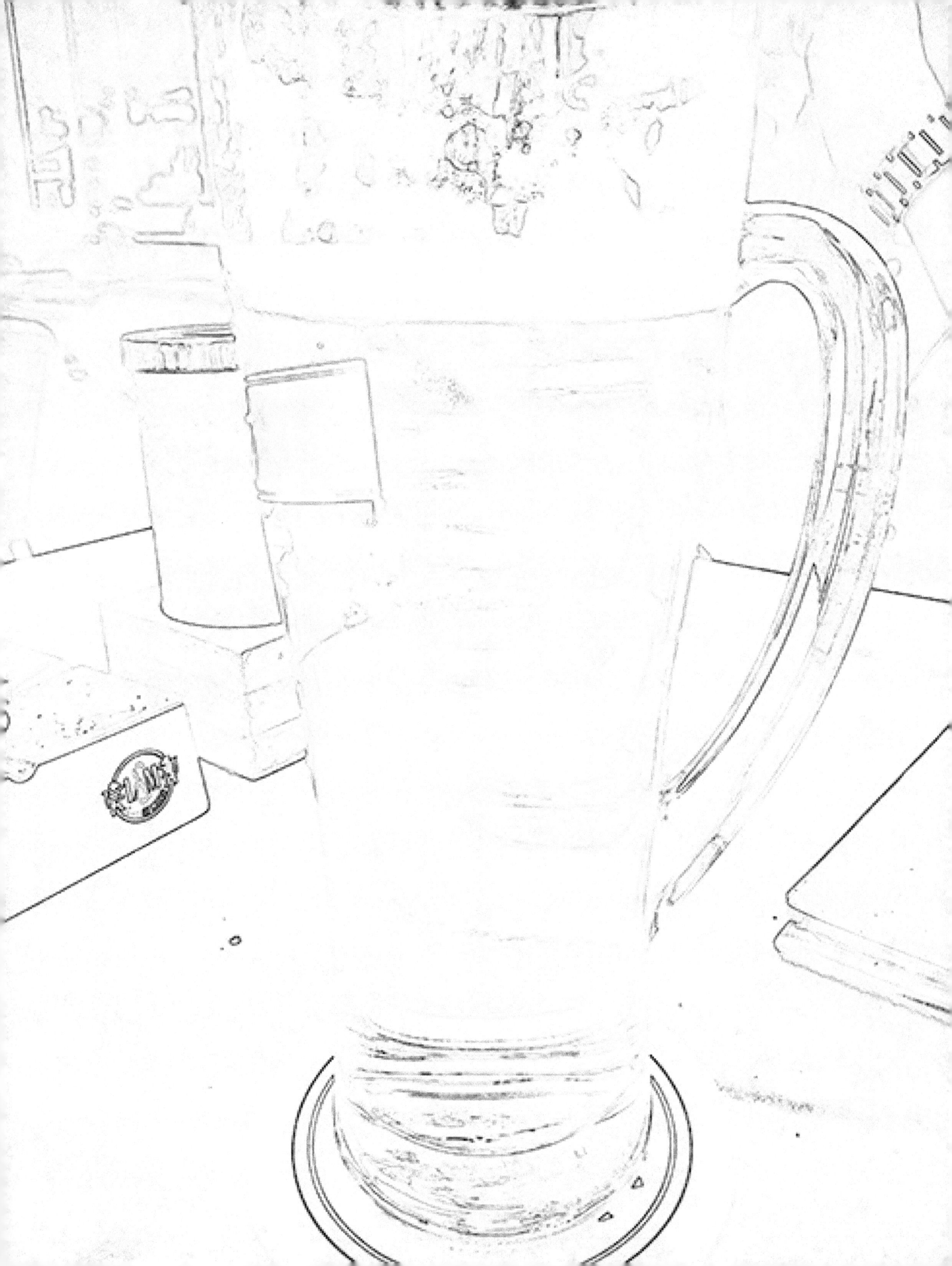

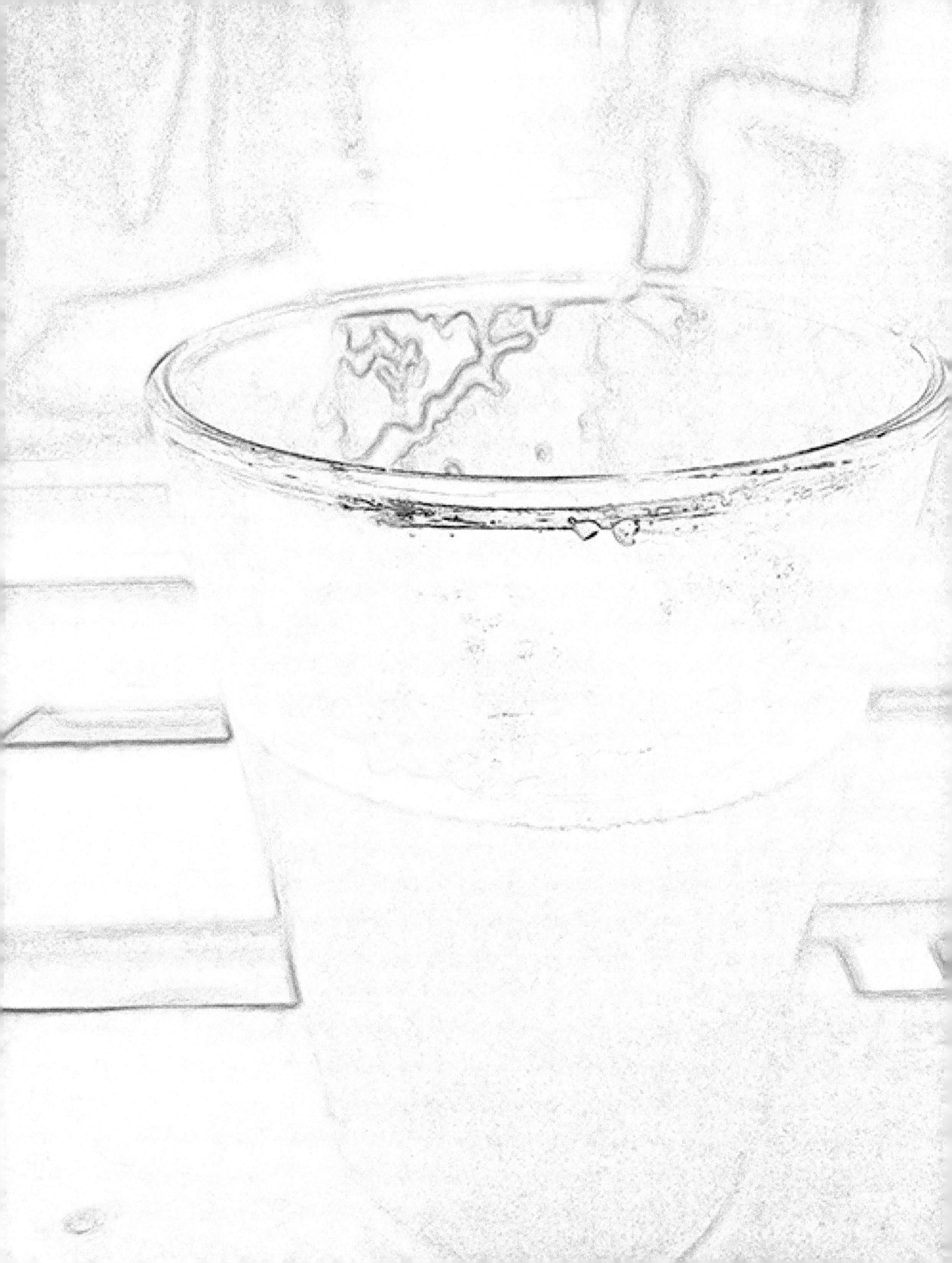

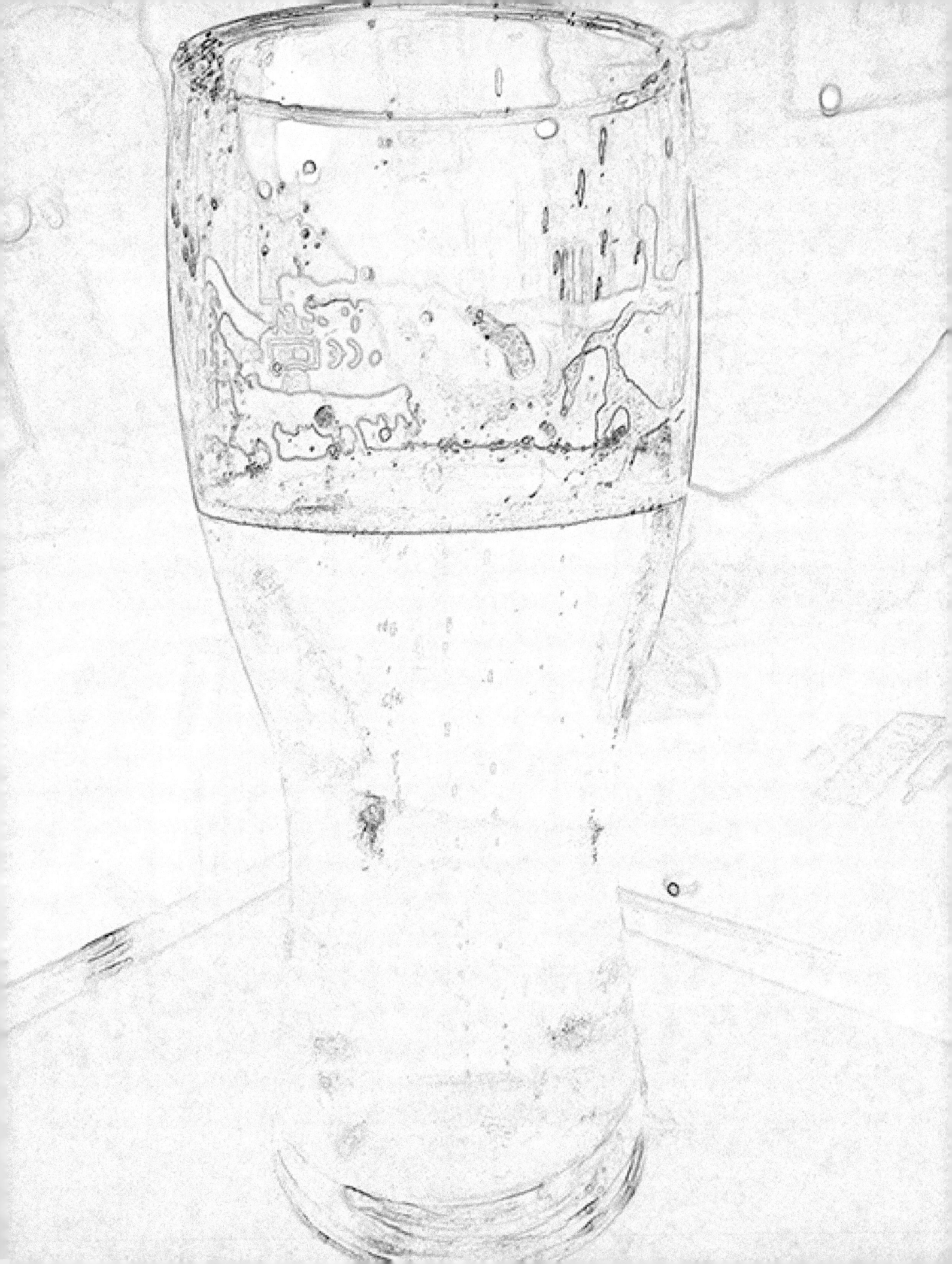

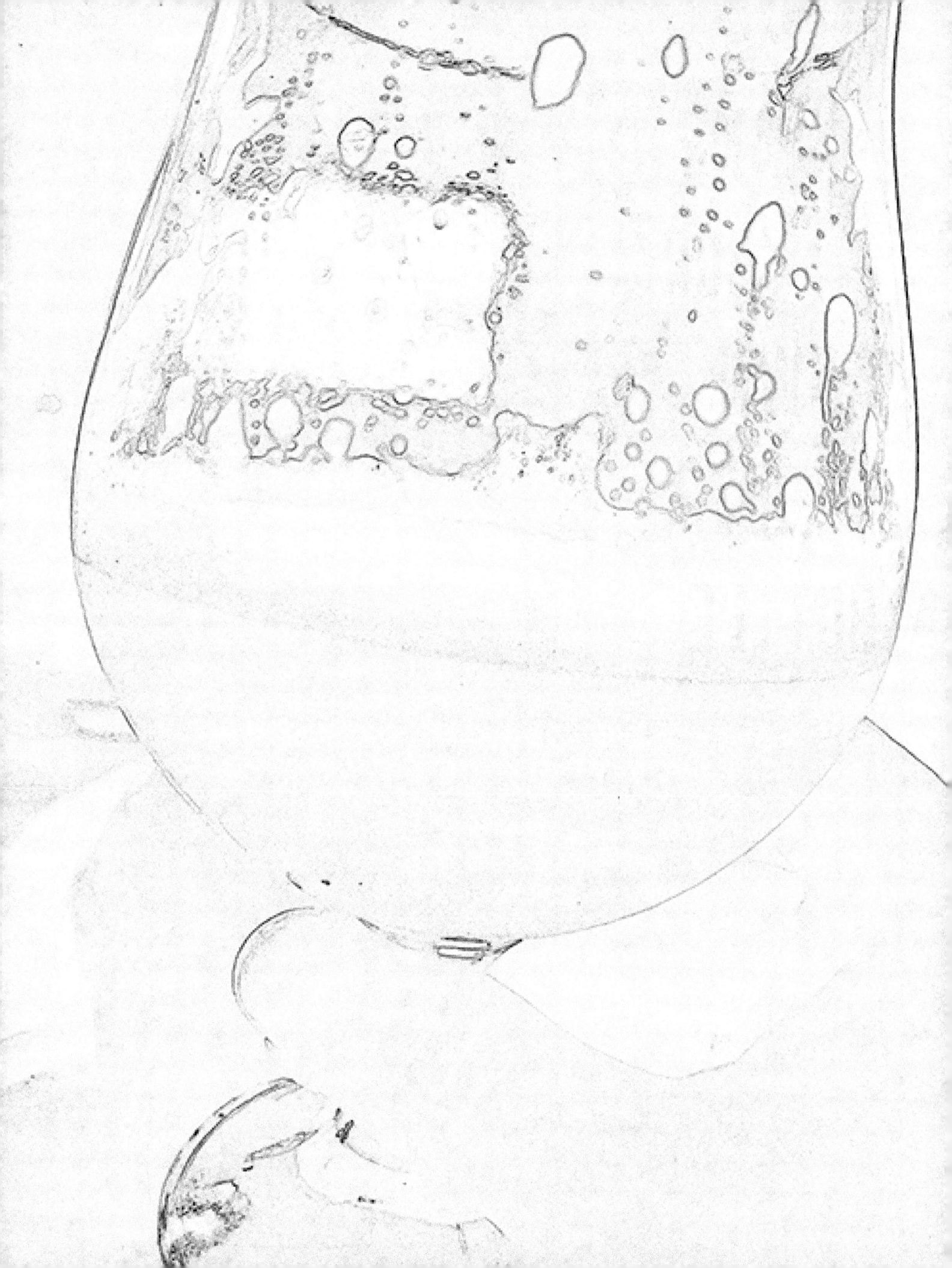

MAKE YOUR OWN BEER BOTTLE

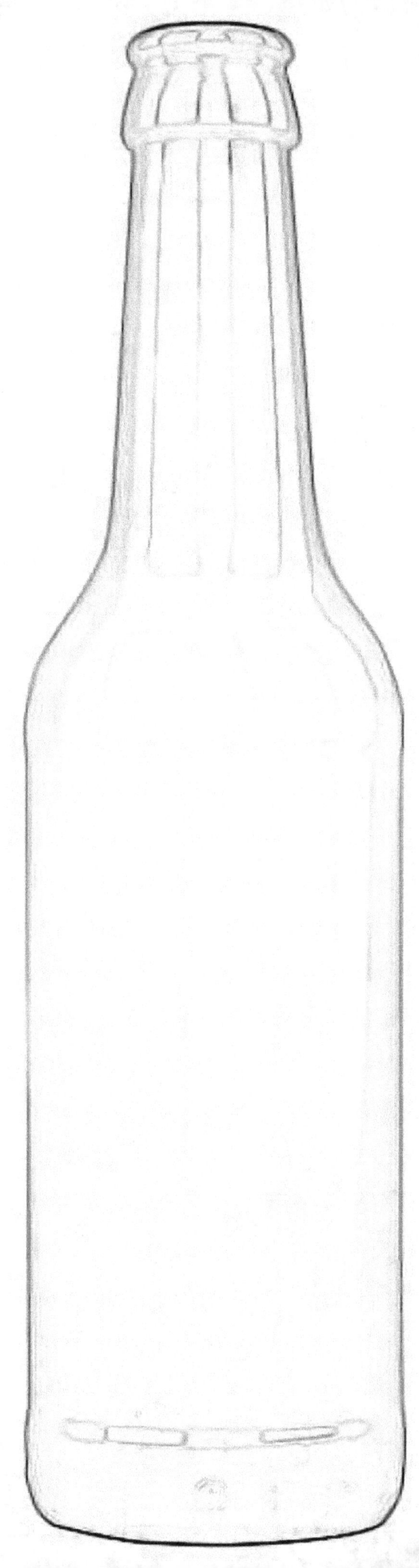

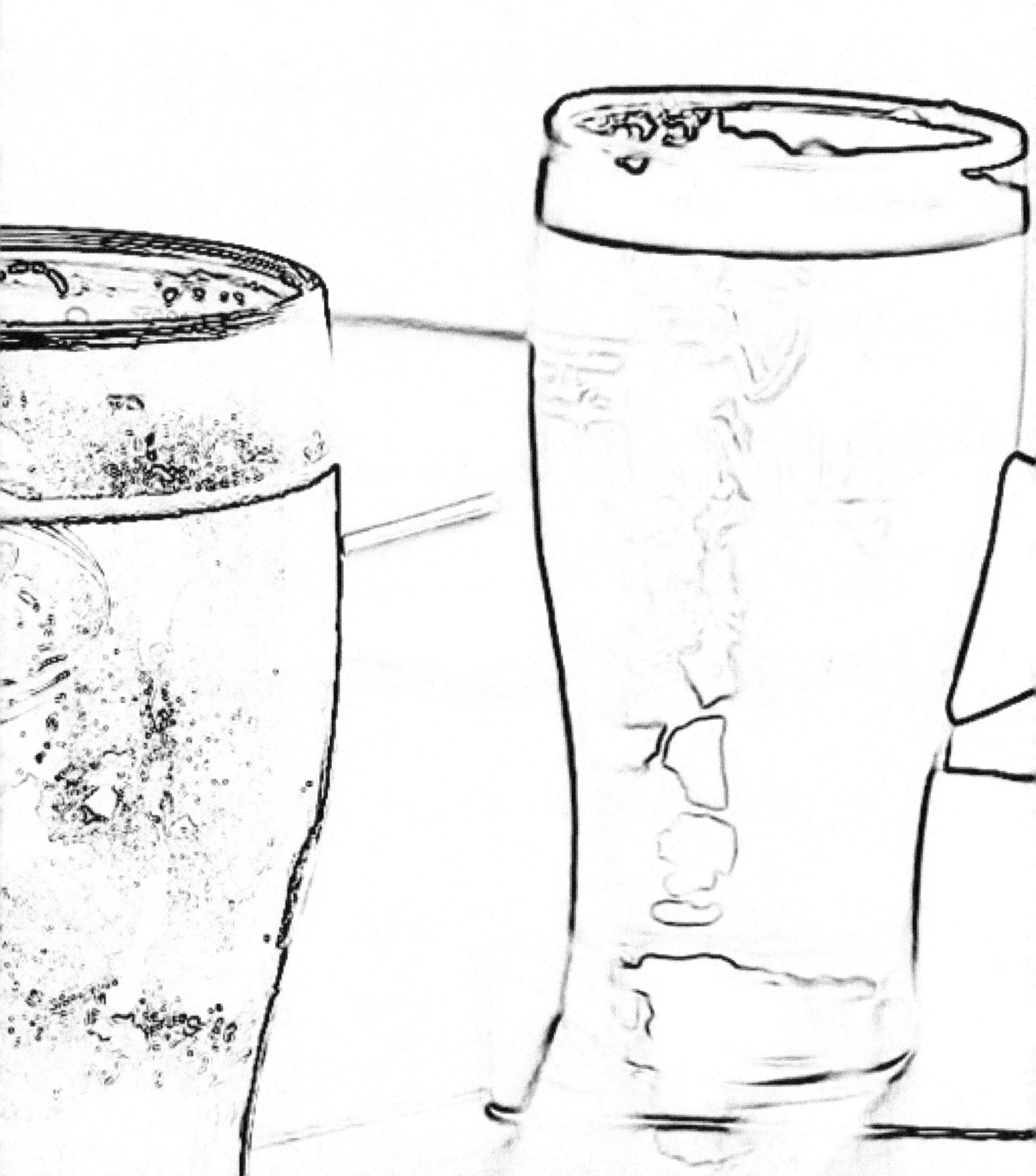

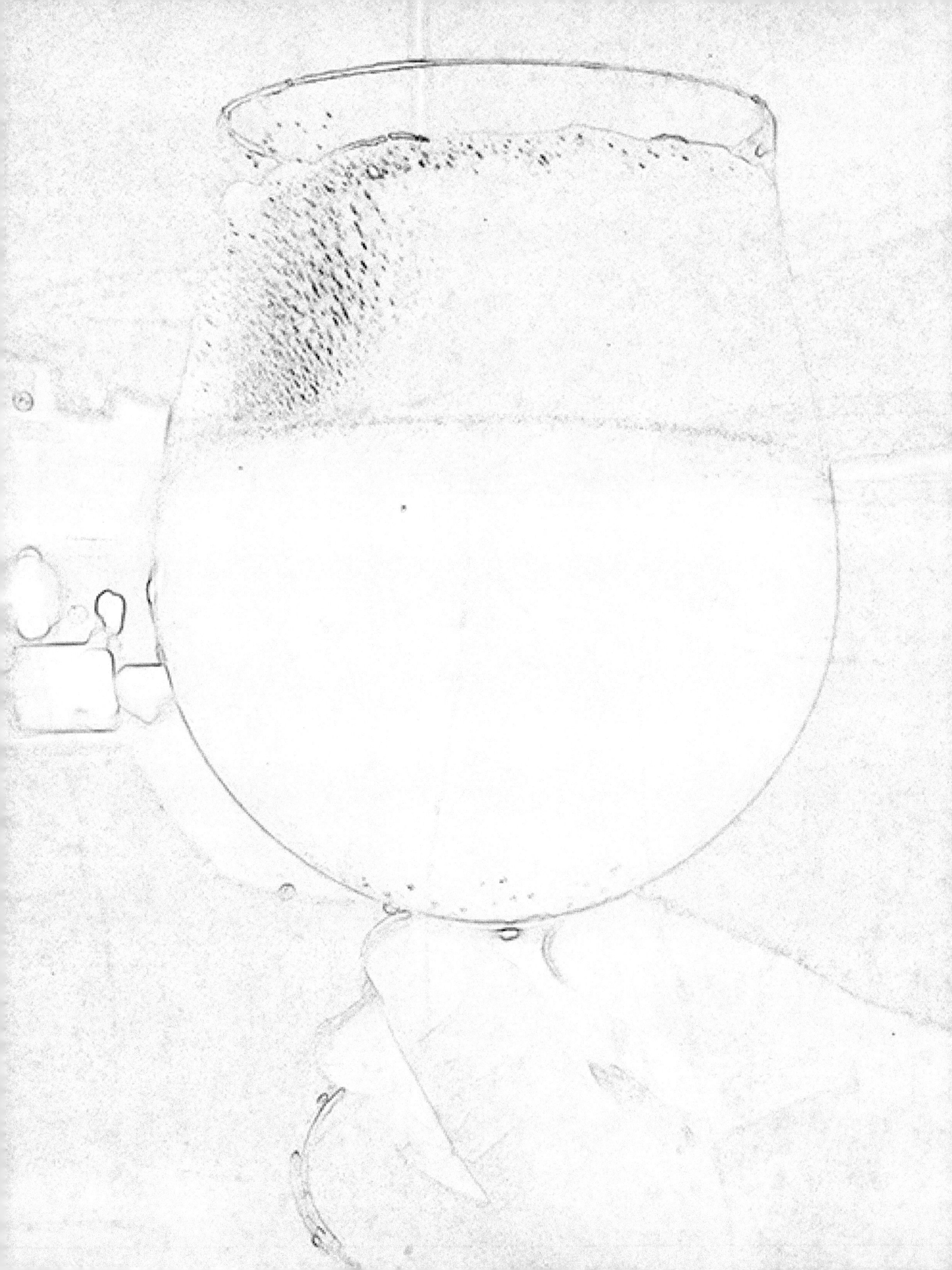

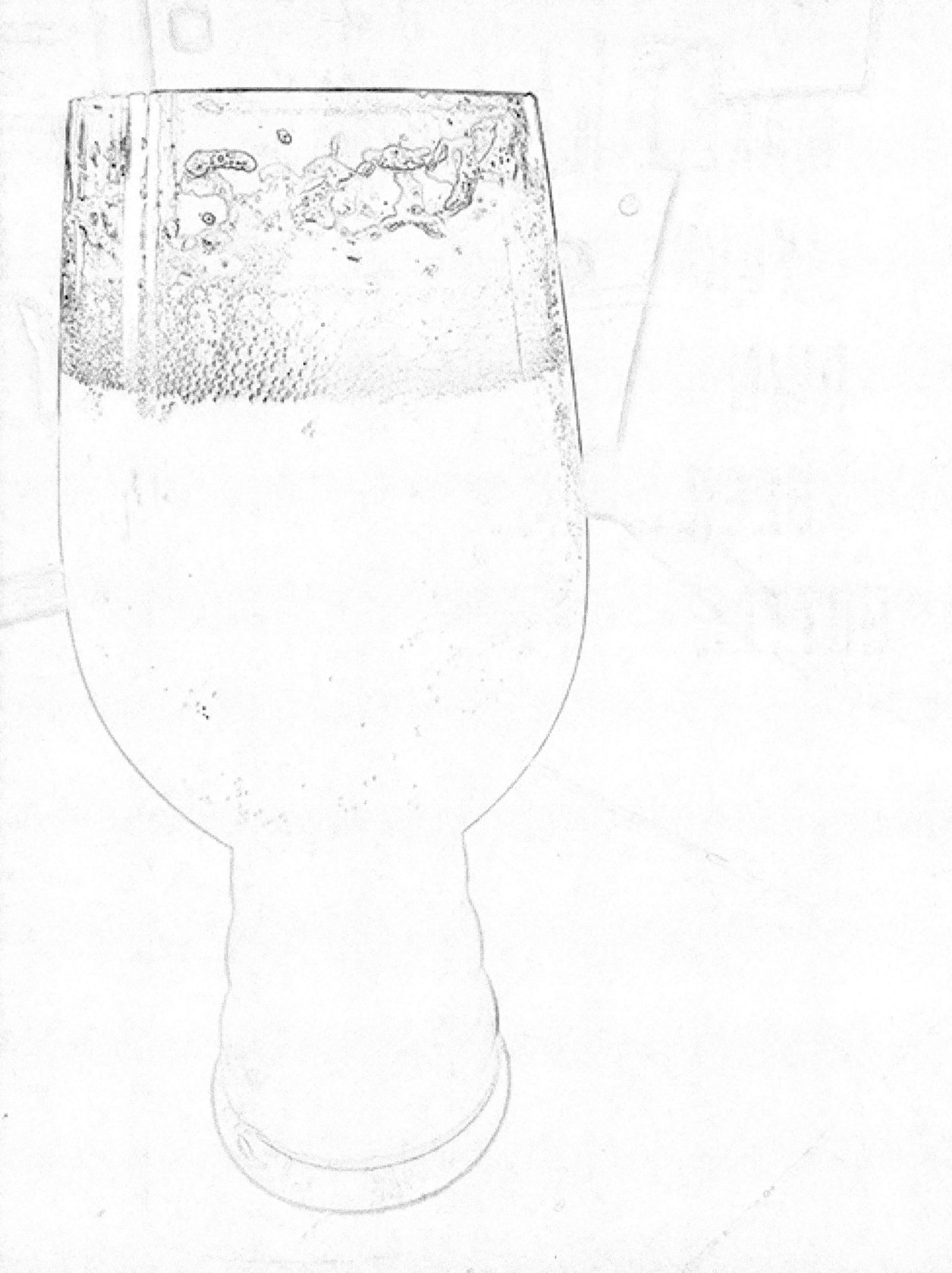

MAKE YOUR OWN BEER BOTTLE

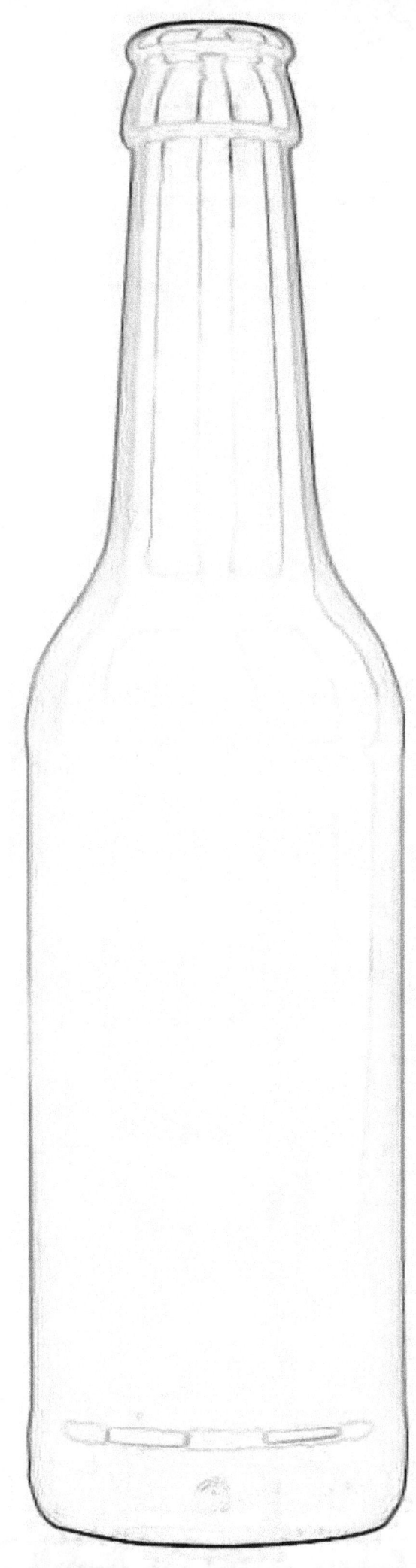

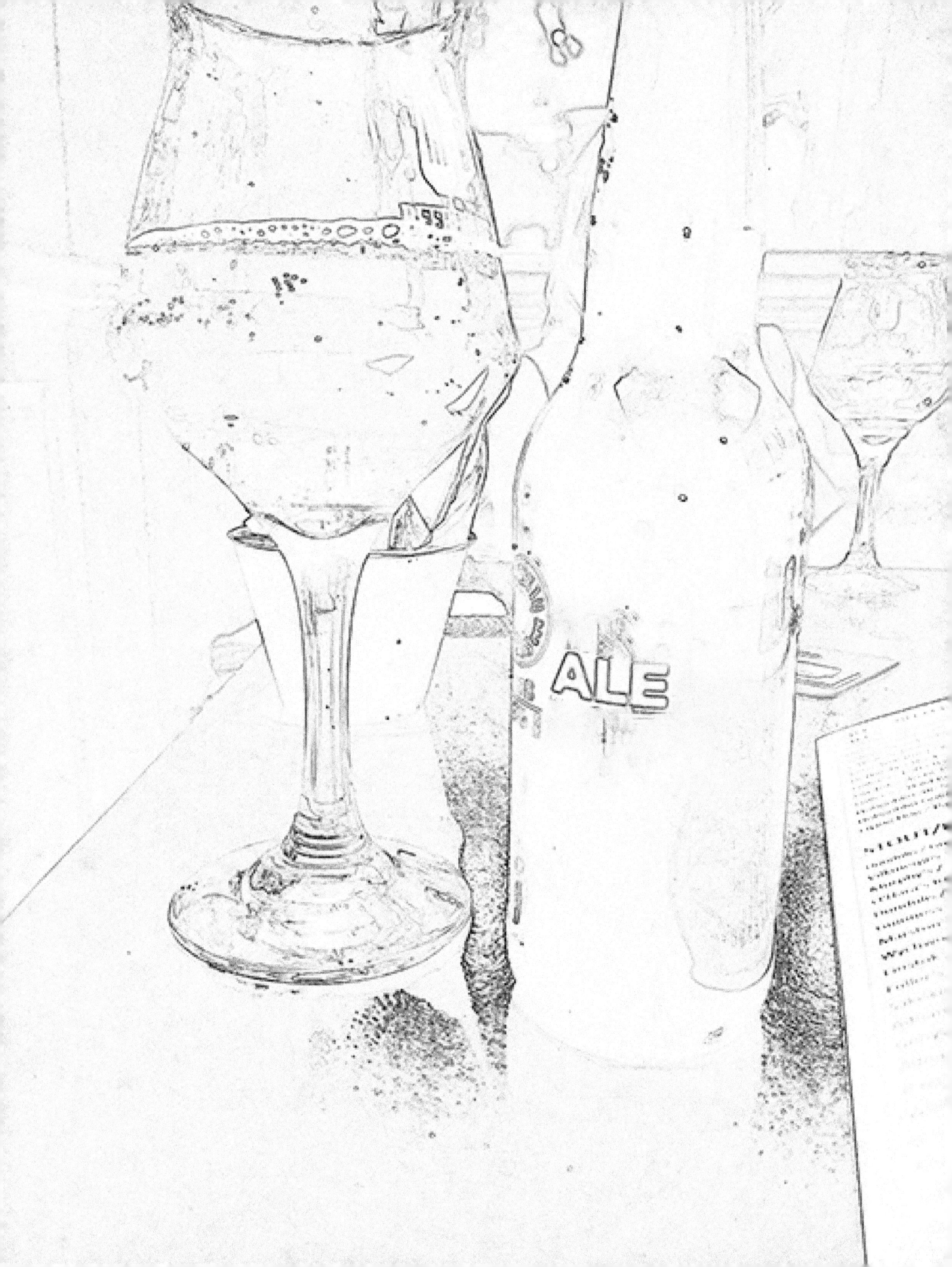

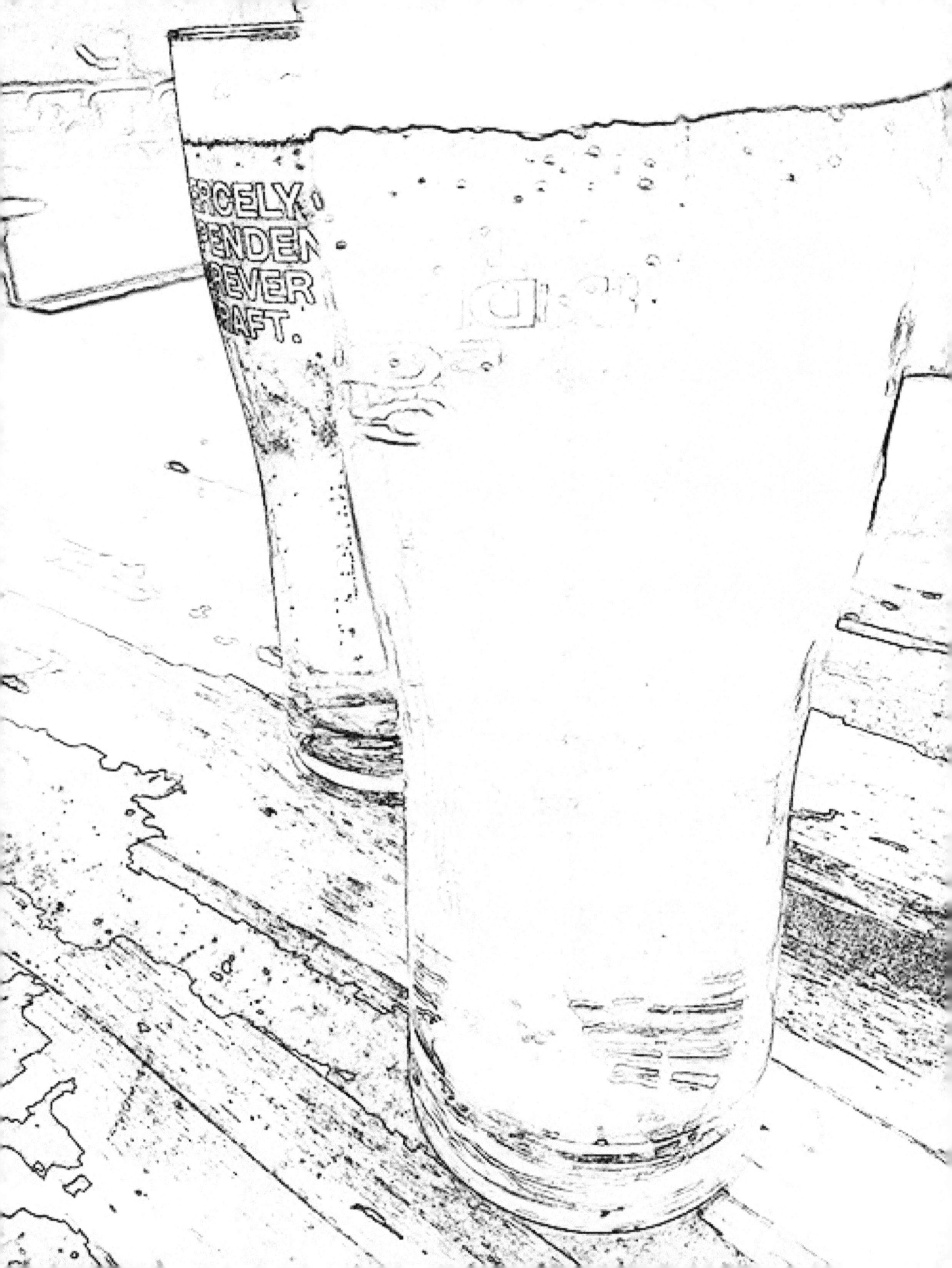

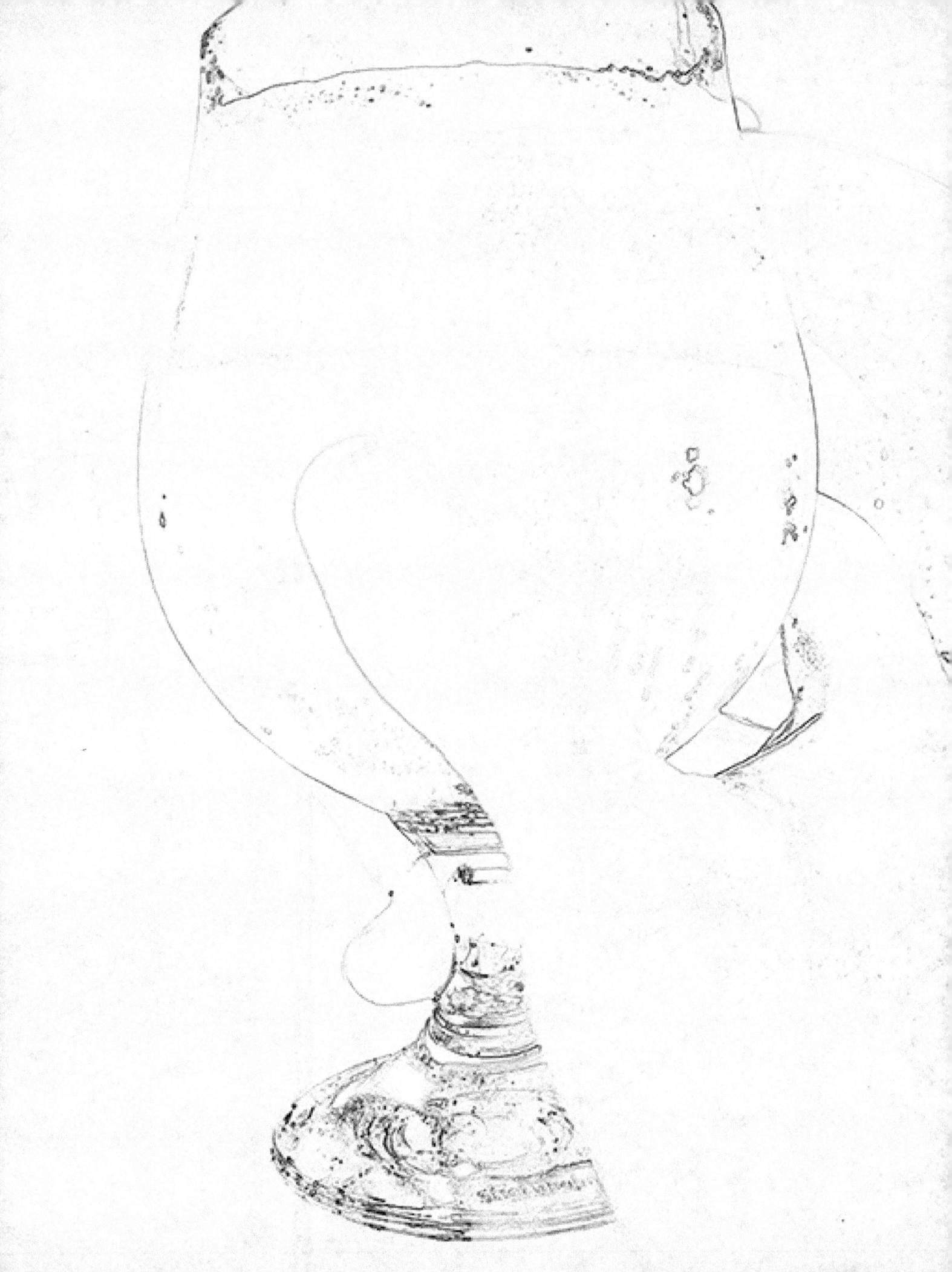

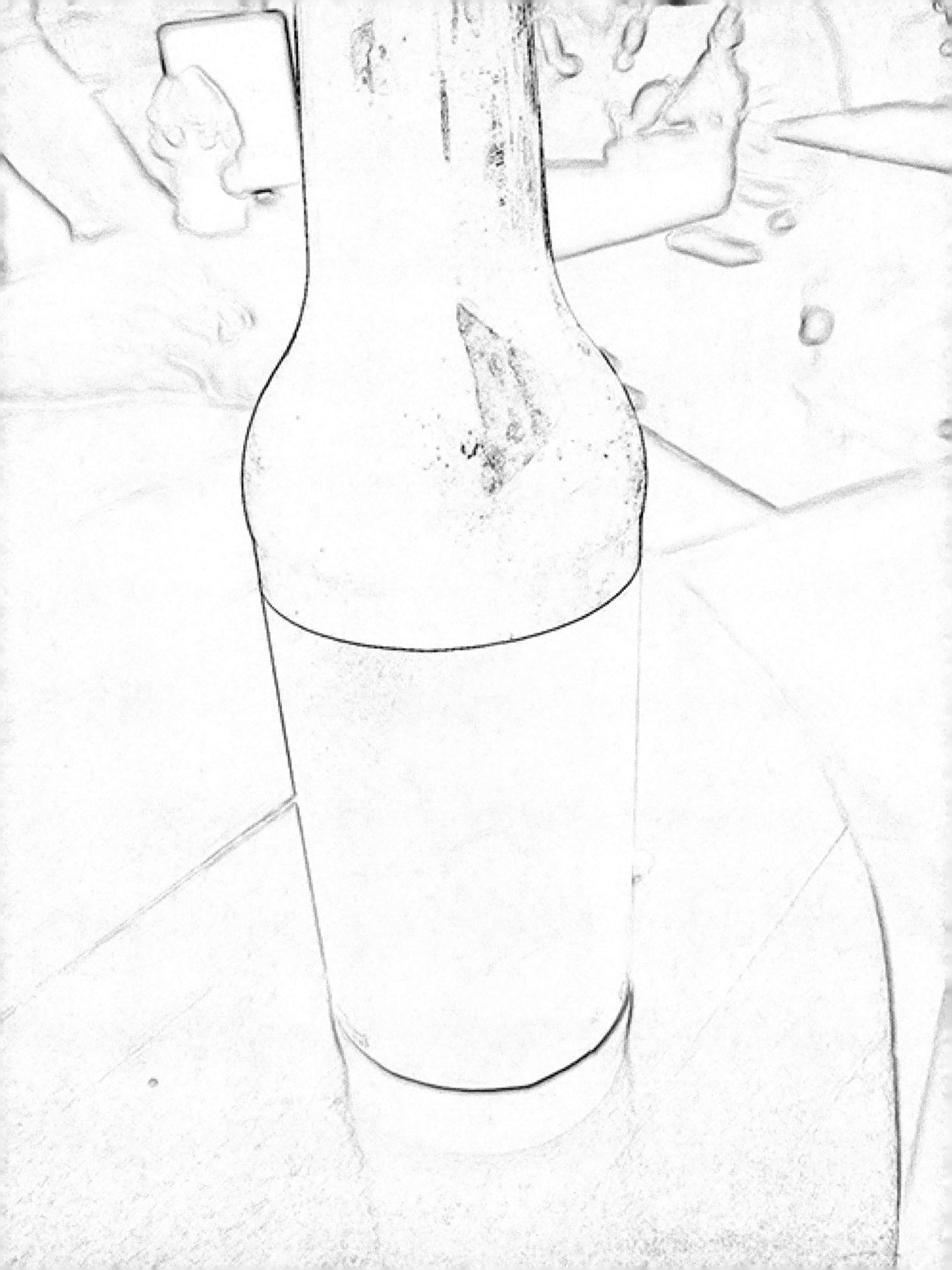

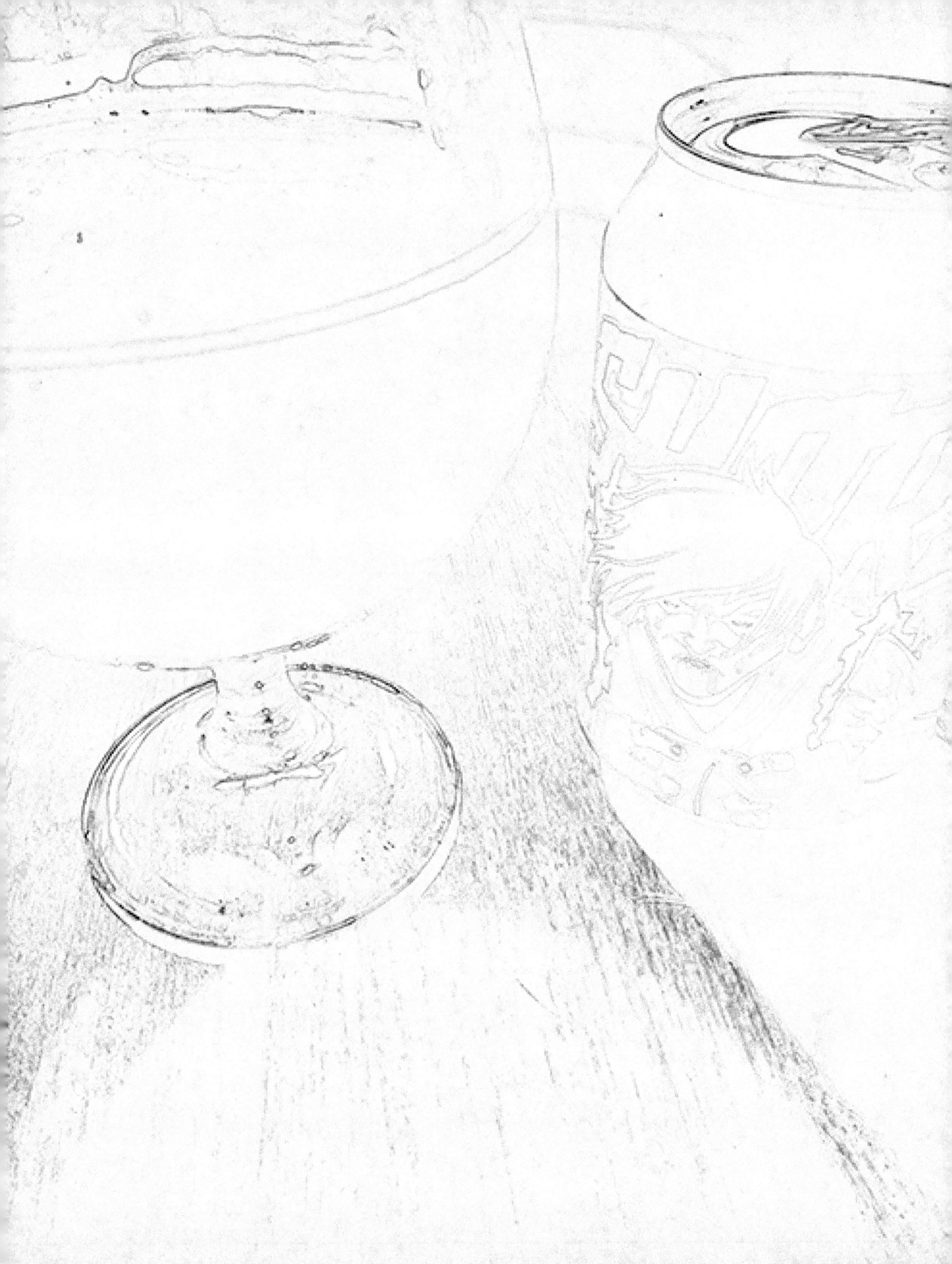

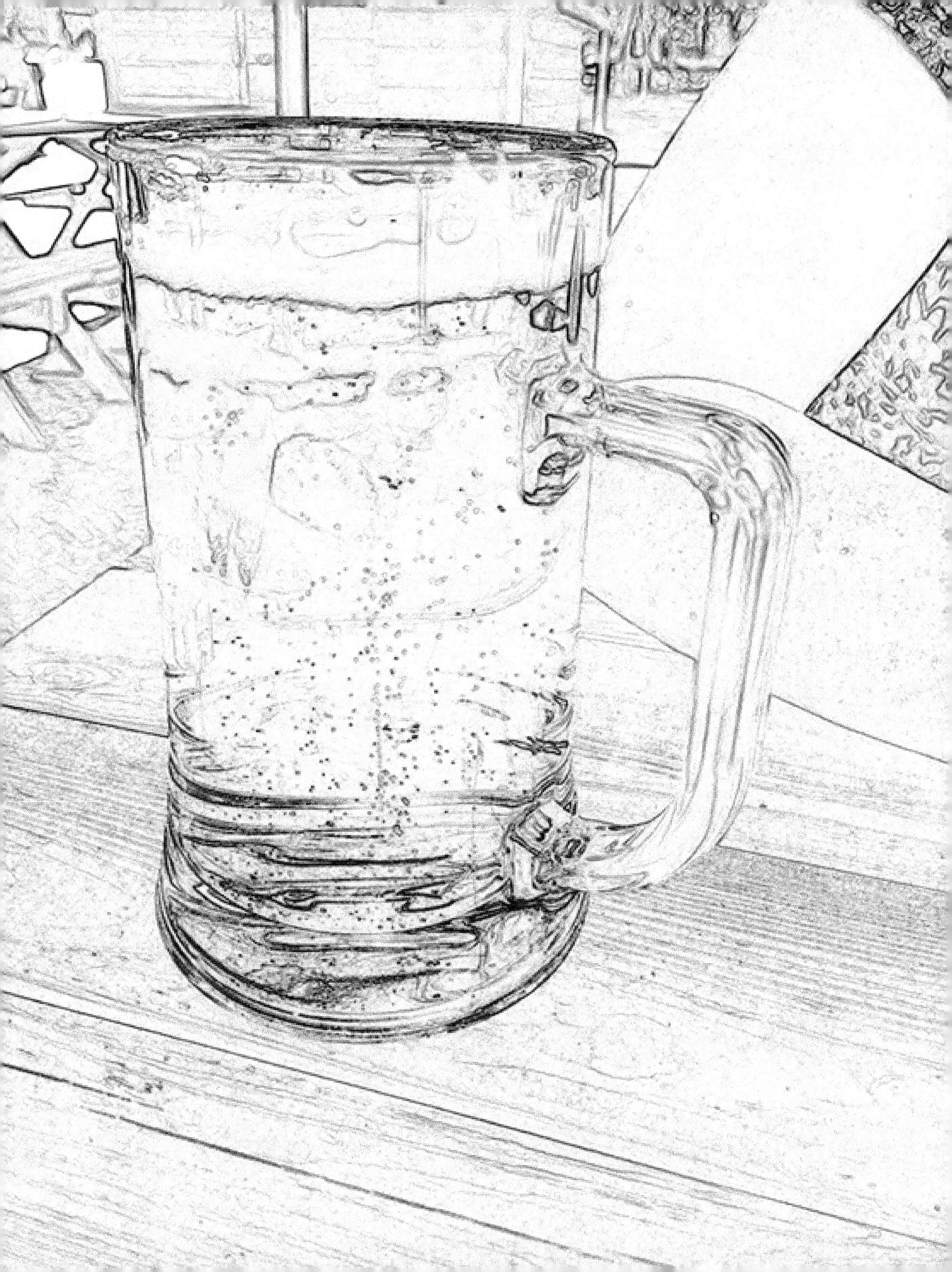

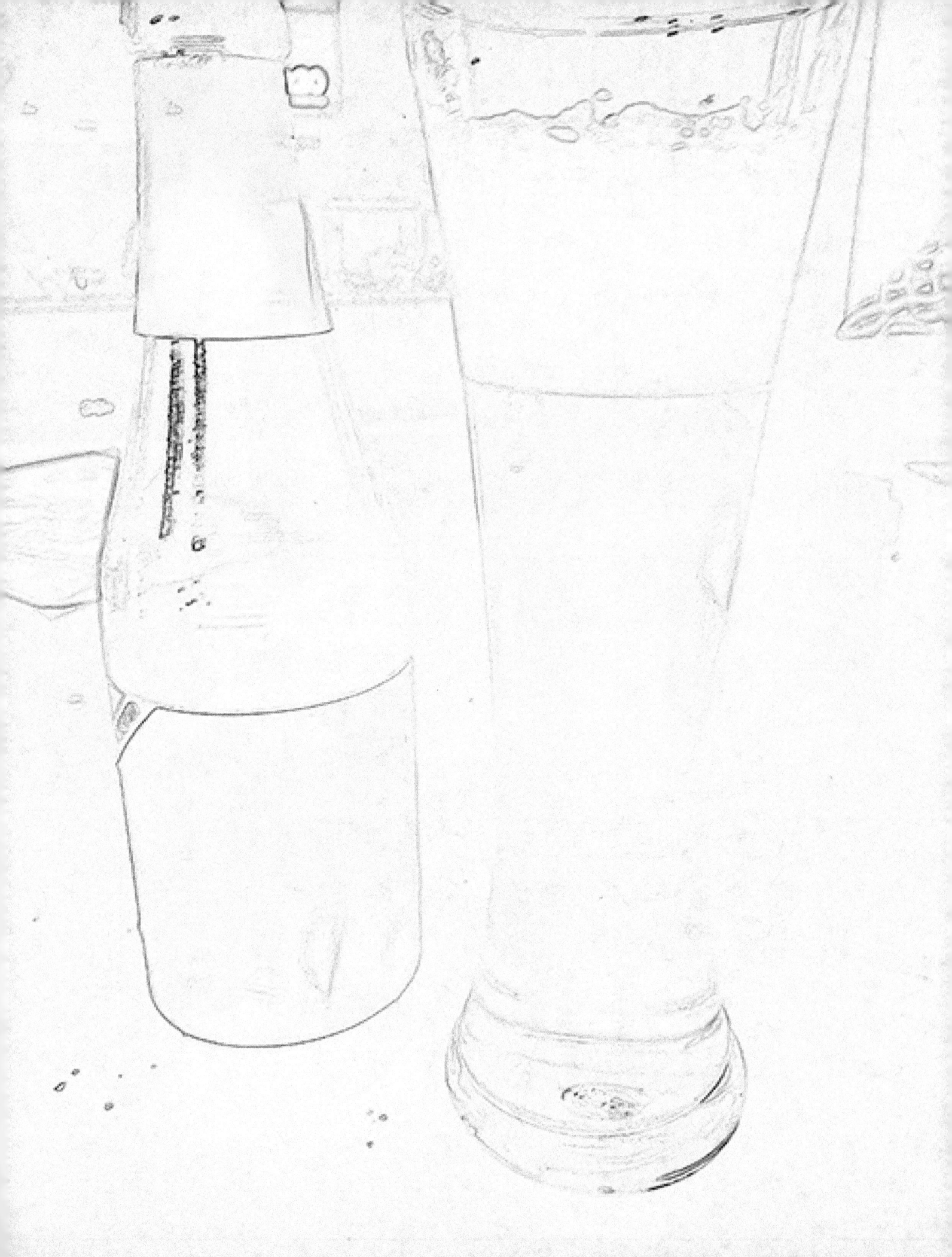

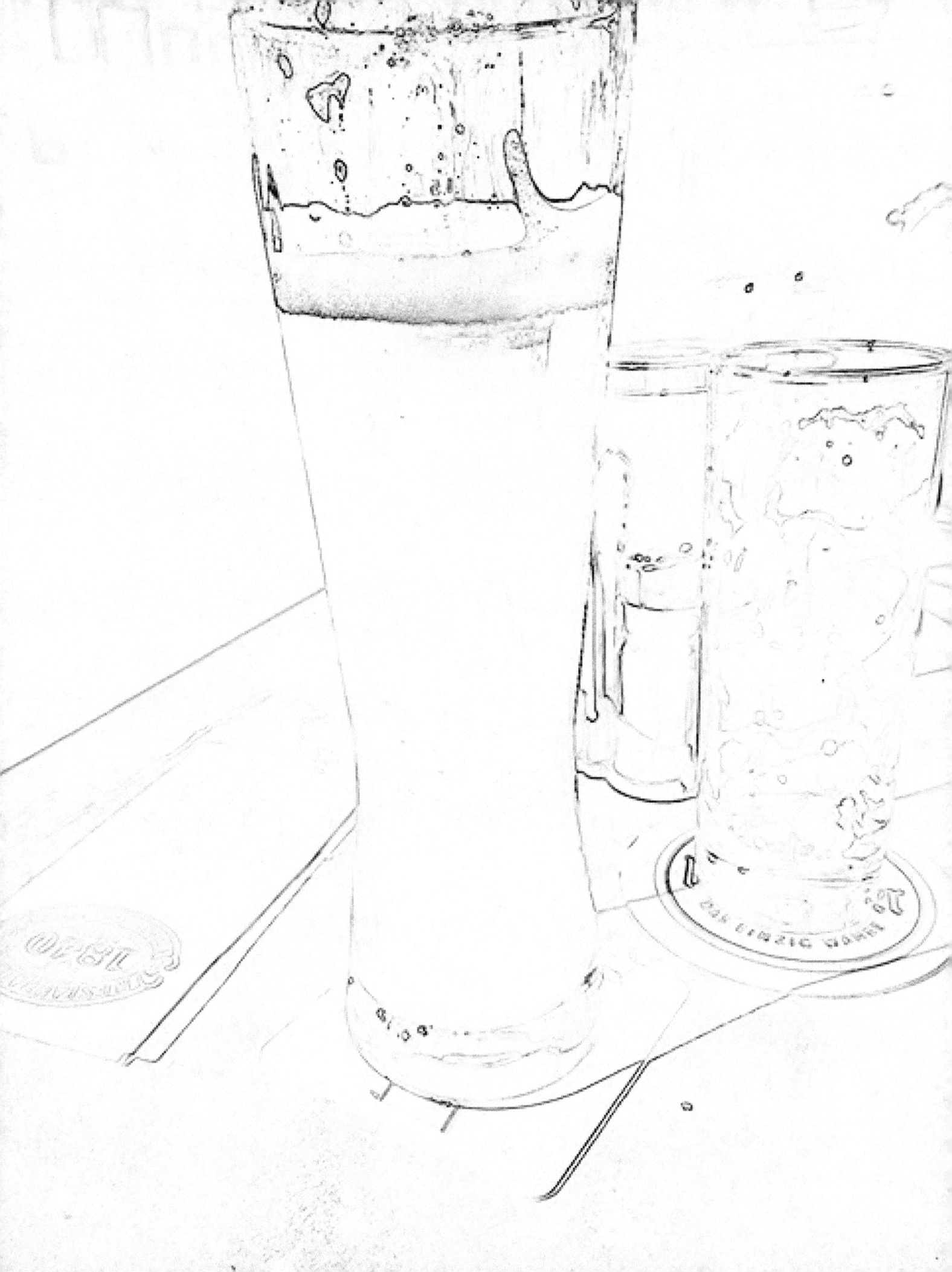

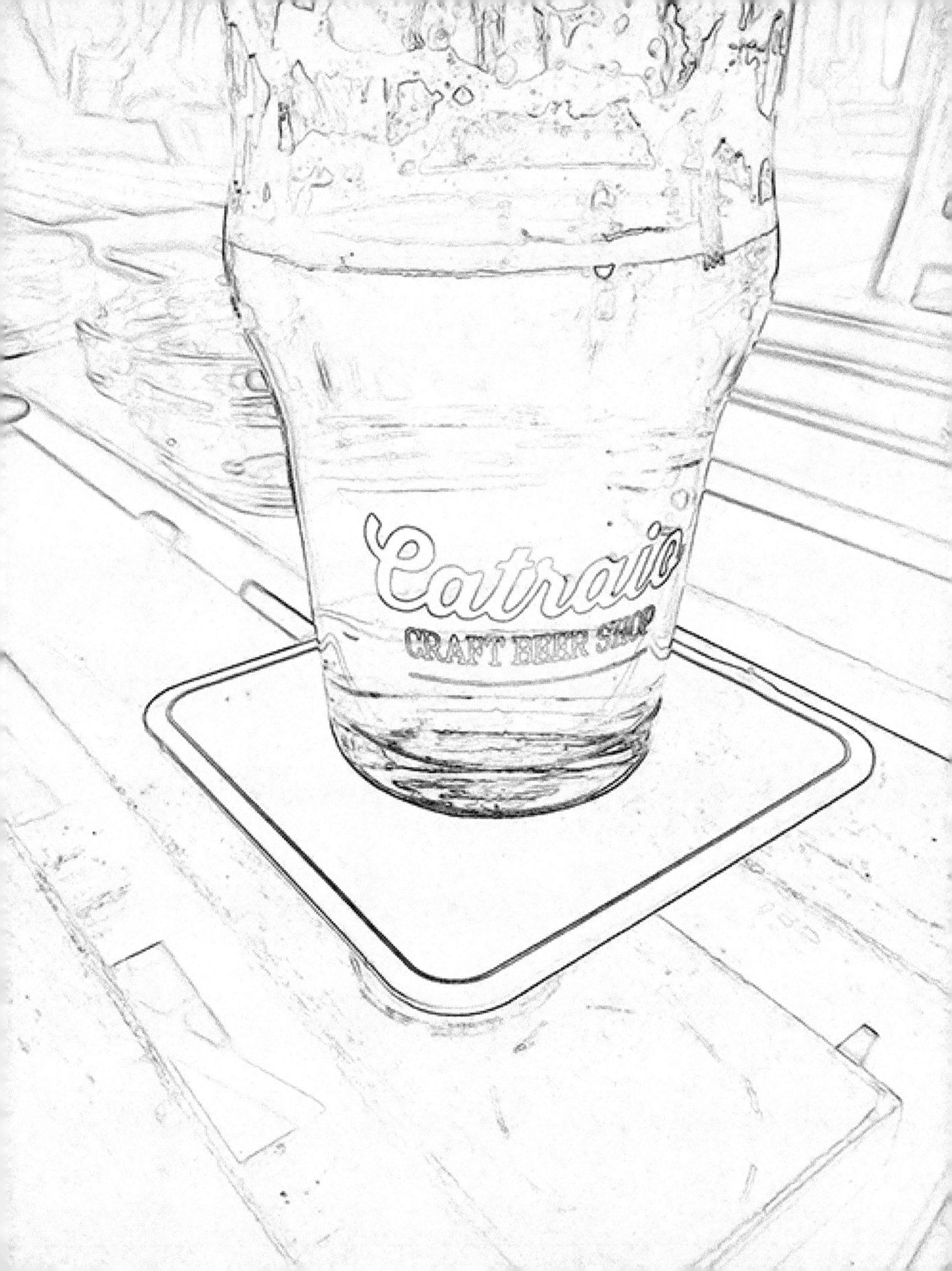

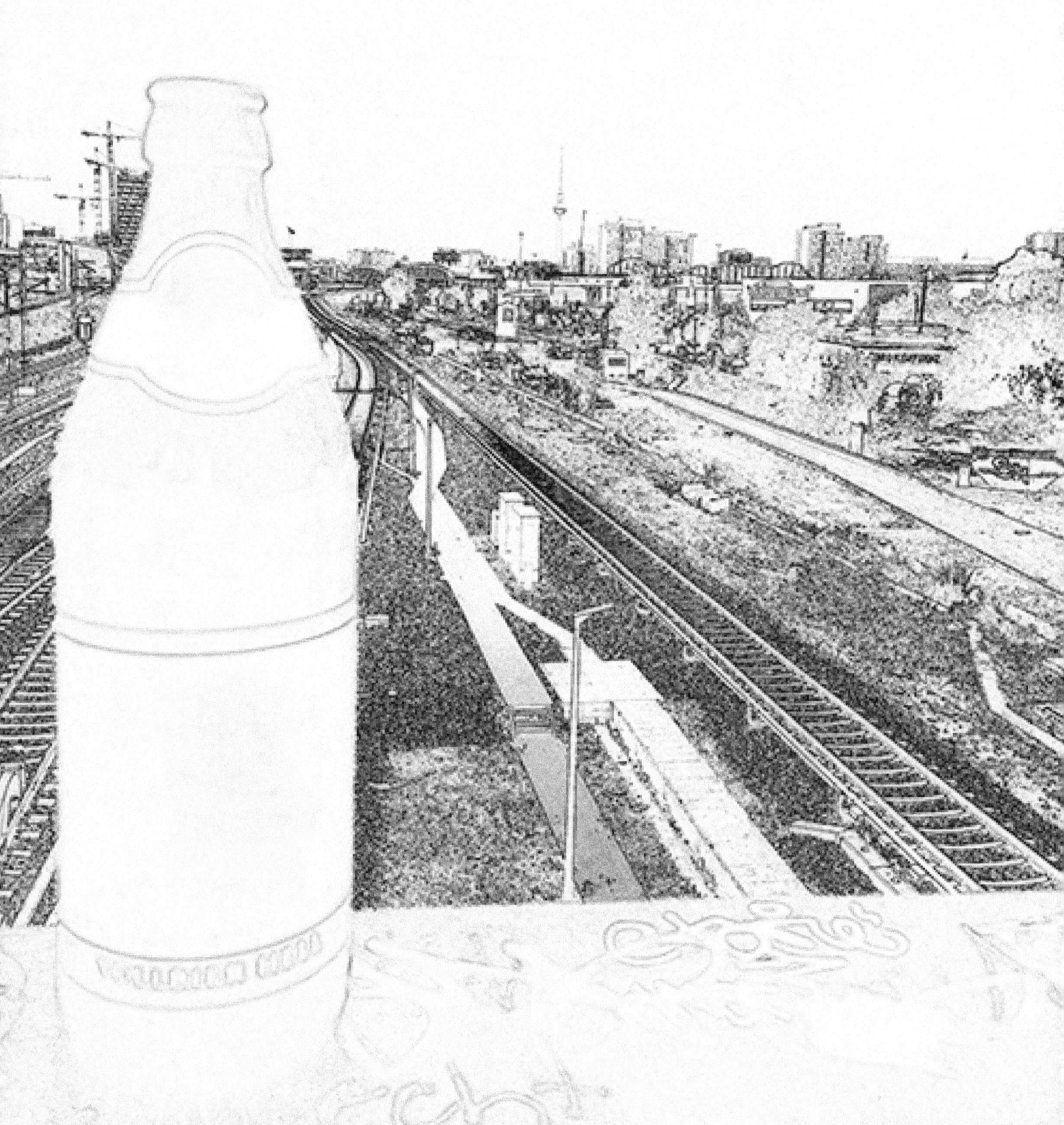

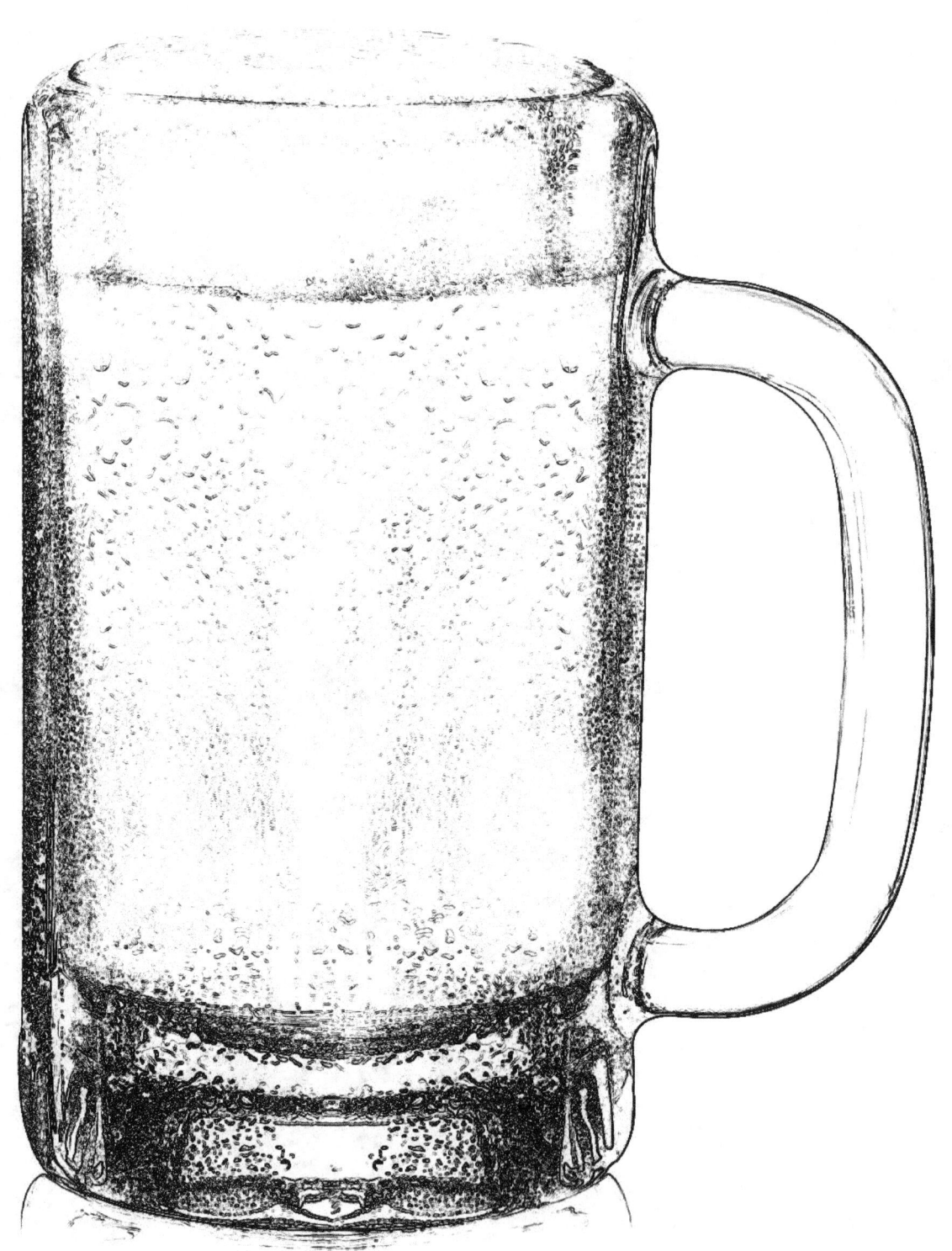

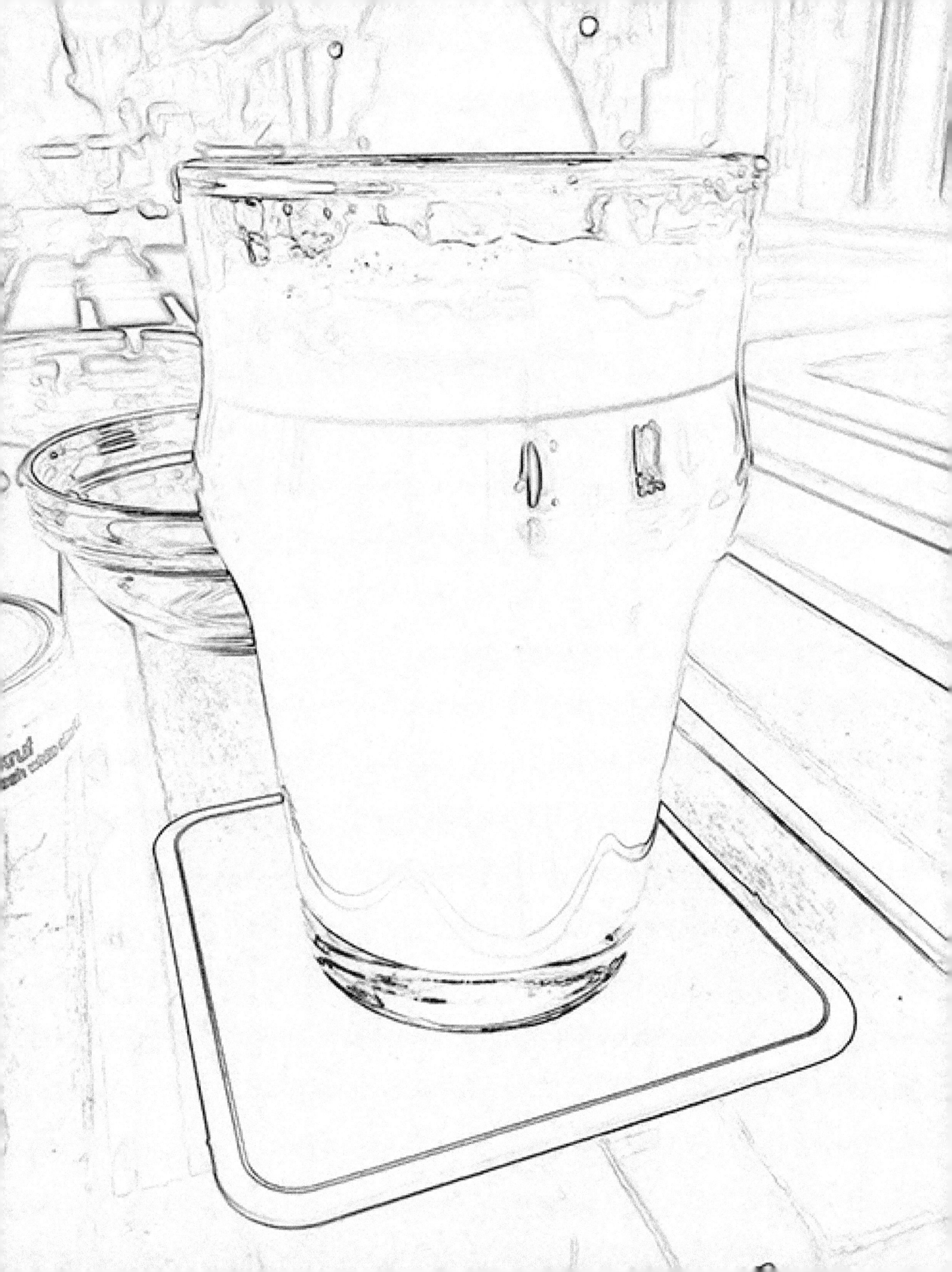

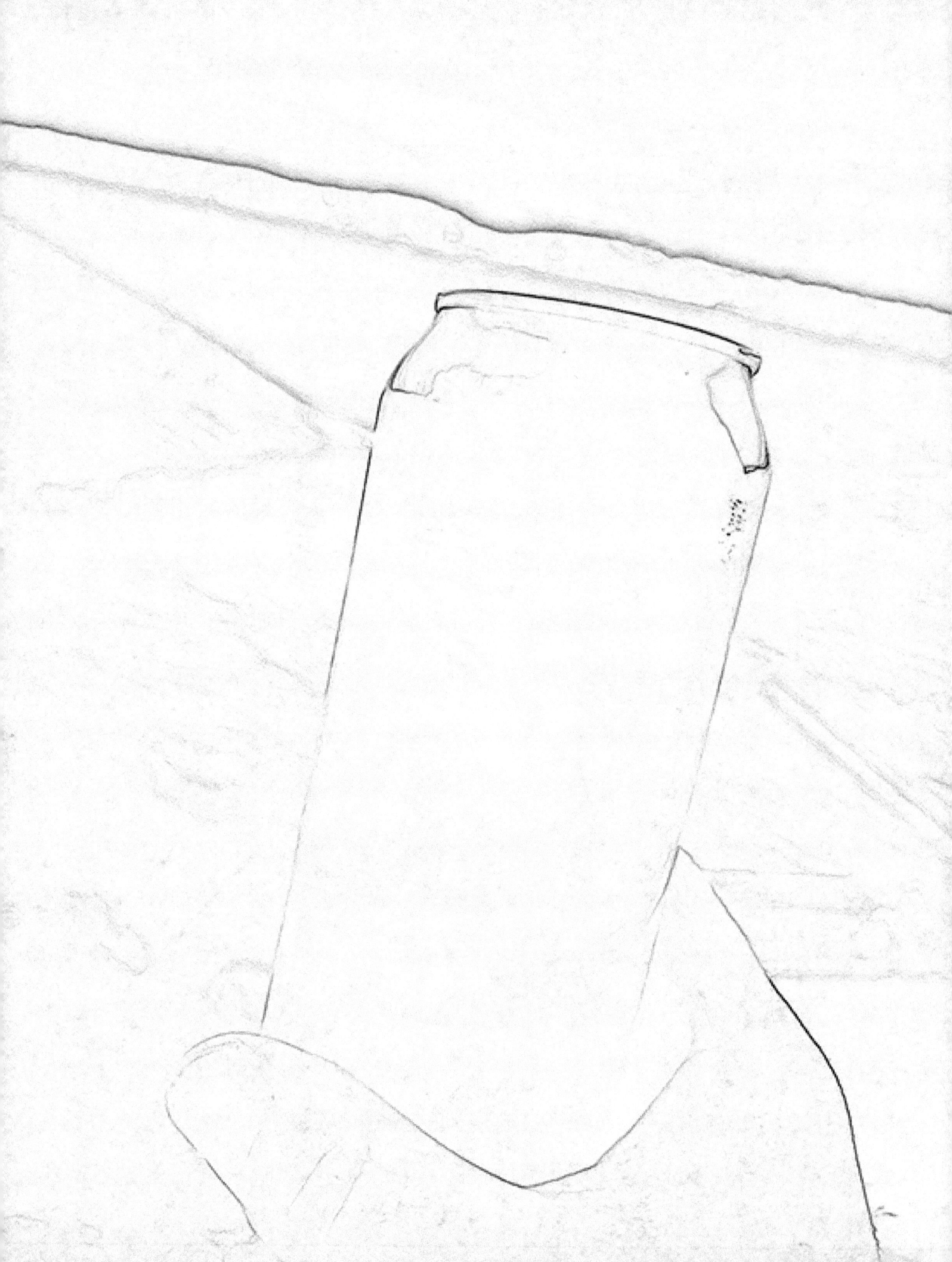

MAKE YOUR OWN BEER LABEL

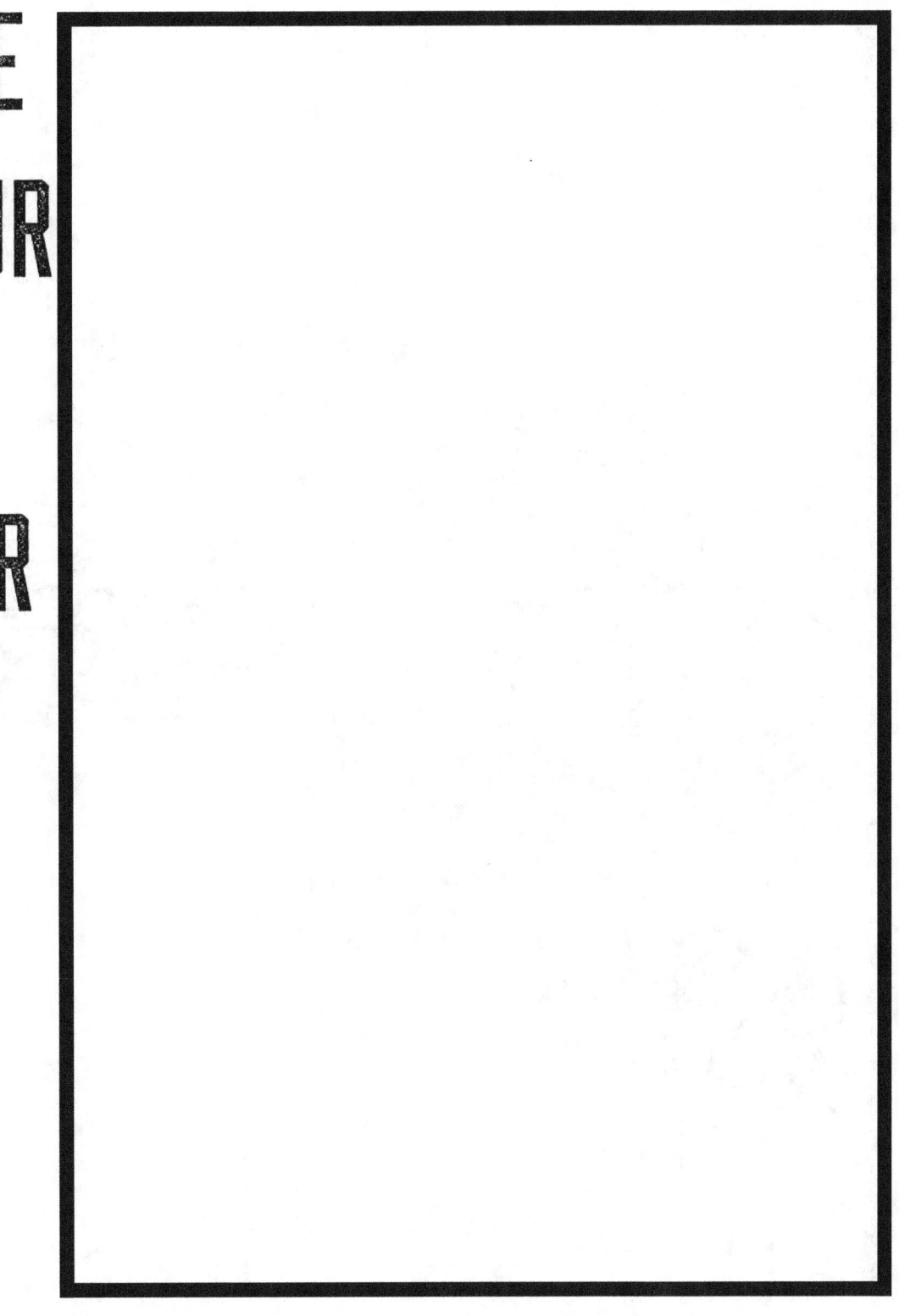

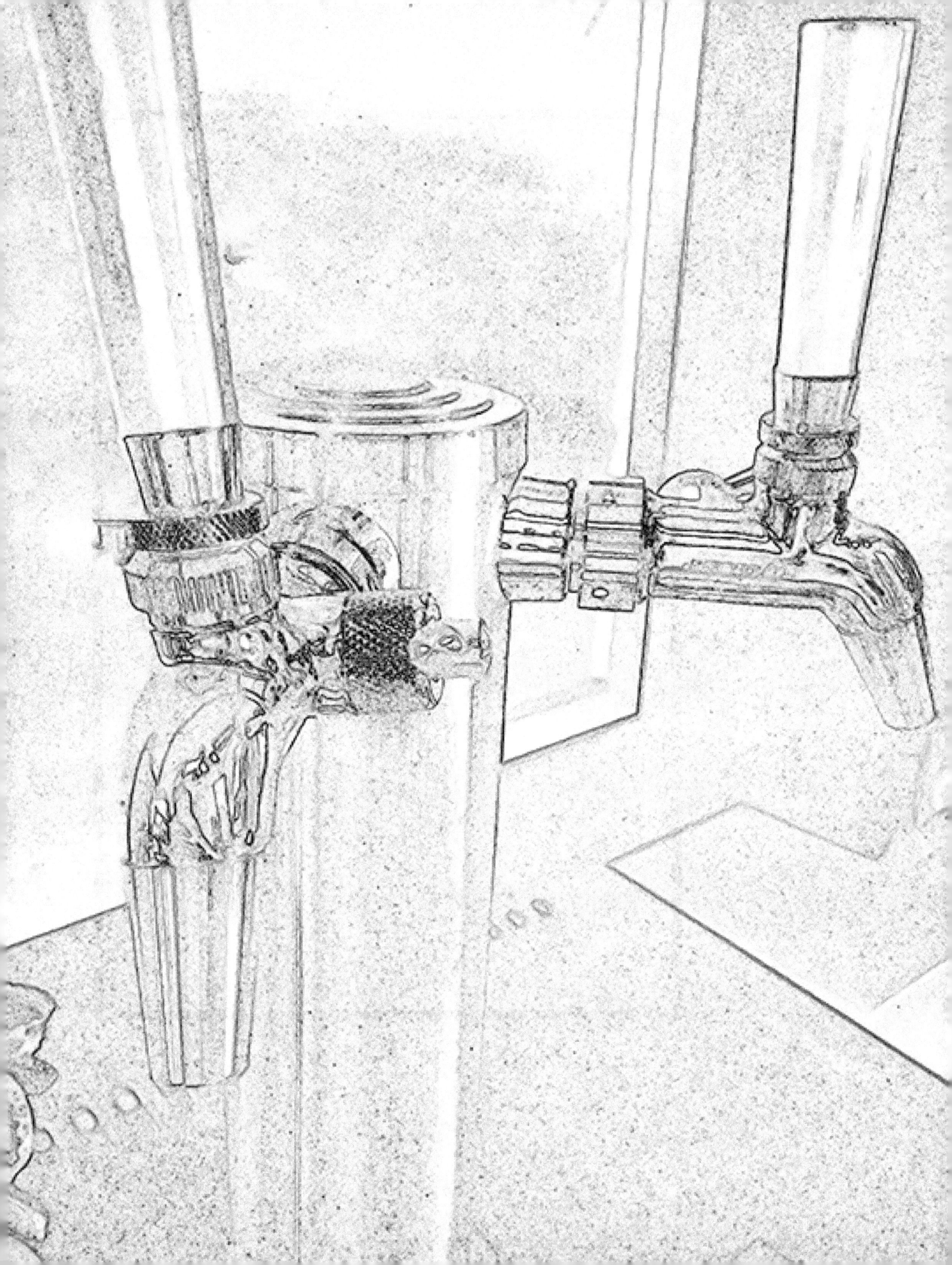

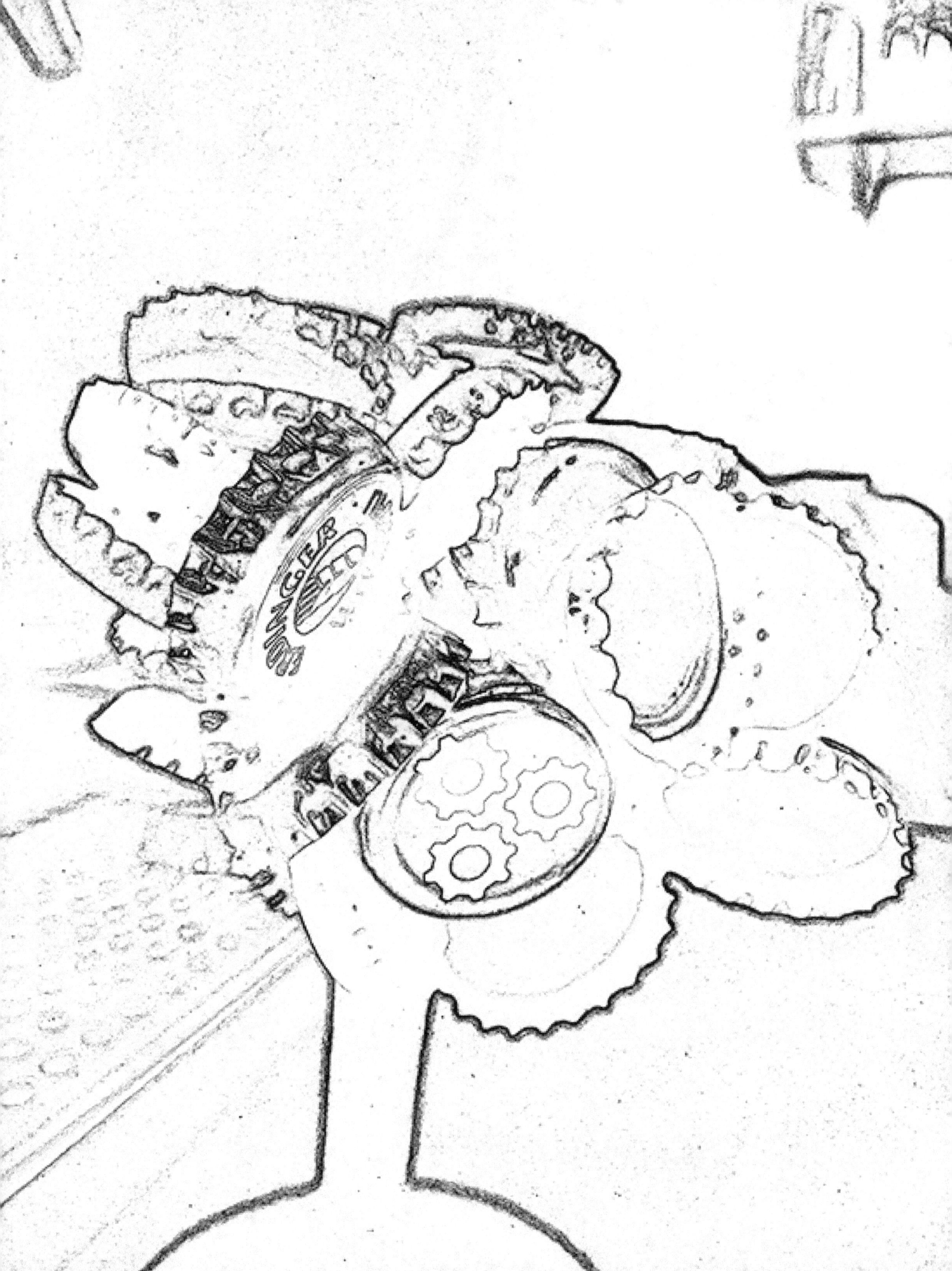

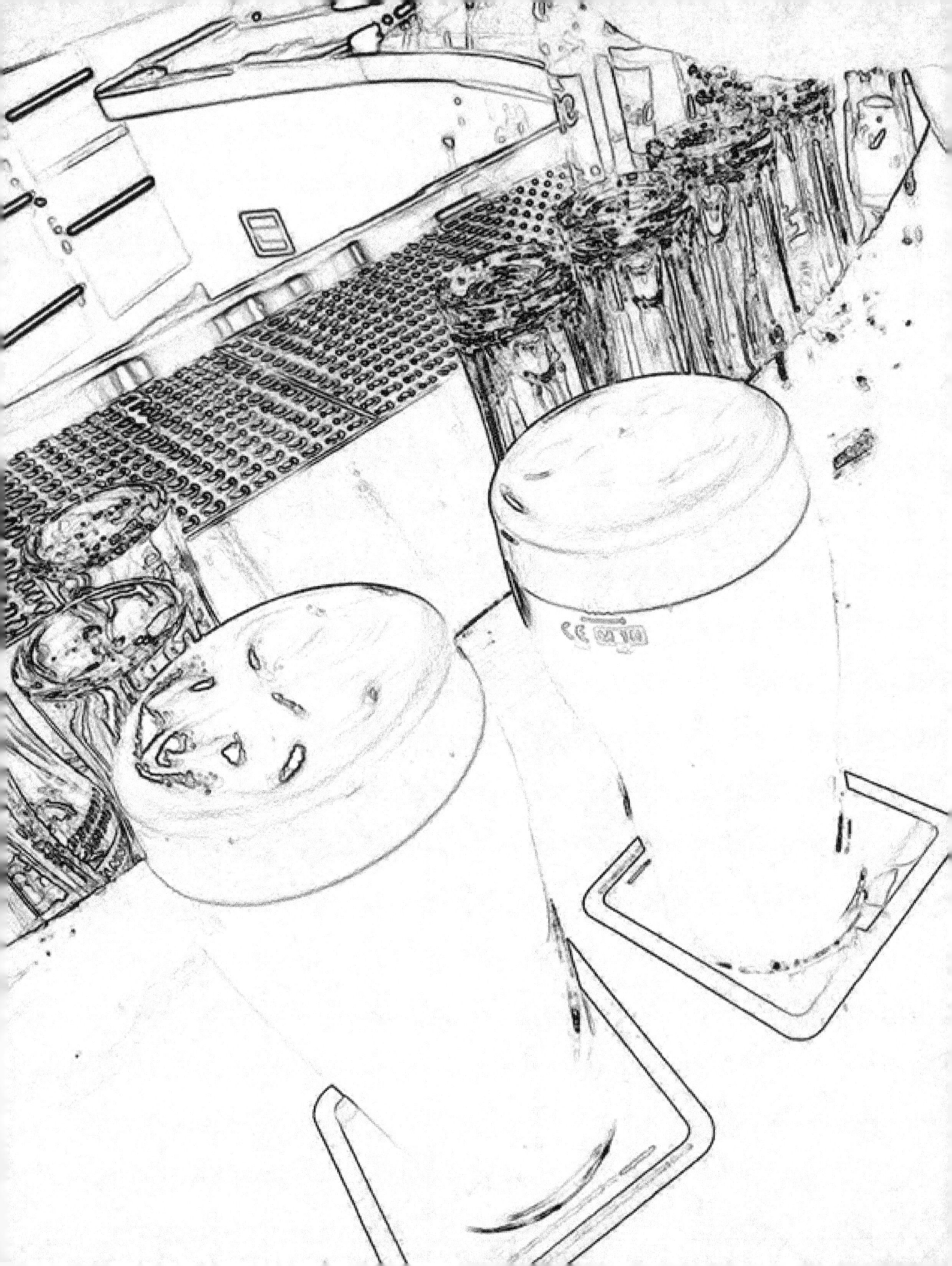

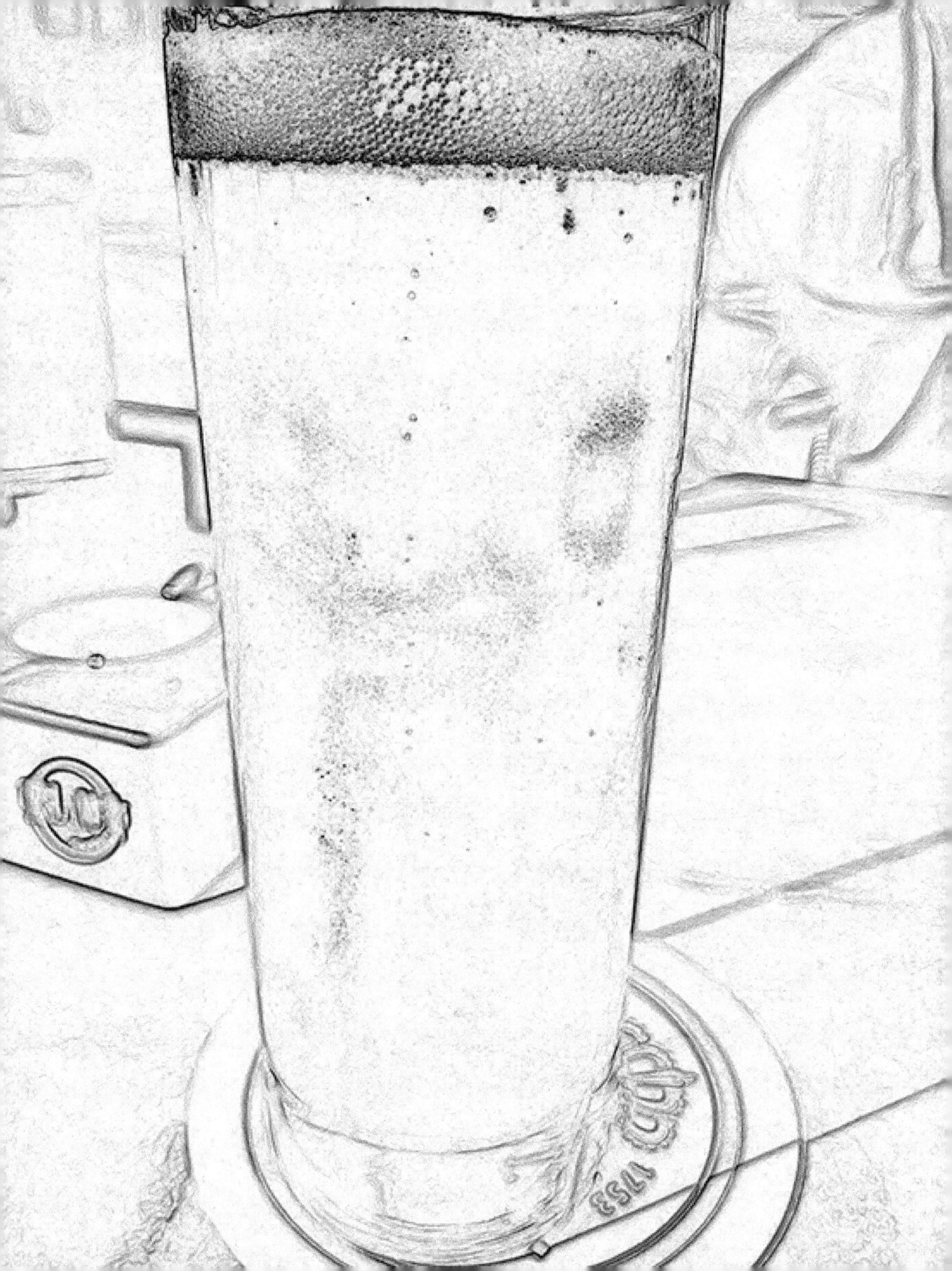

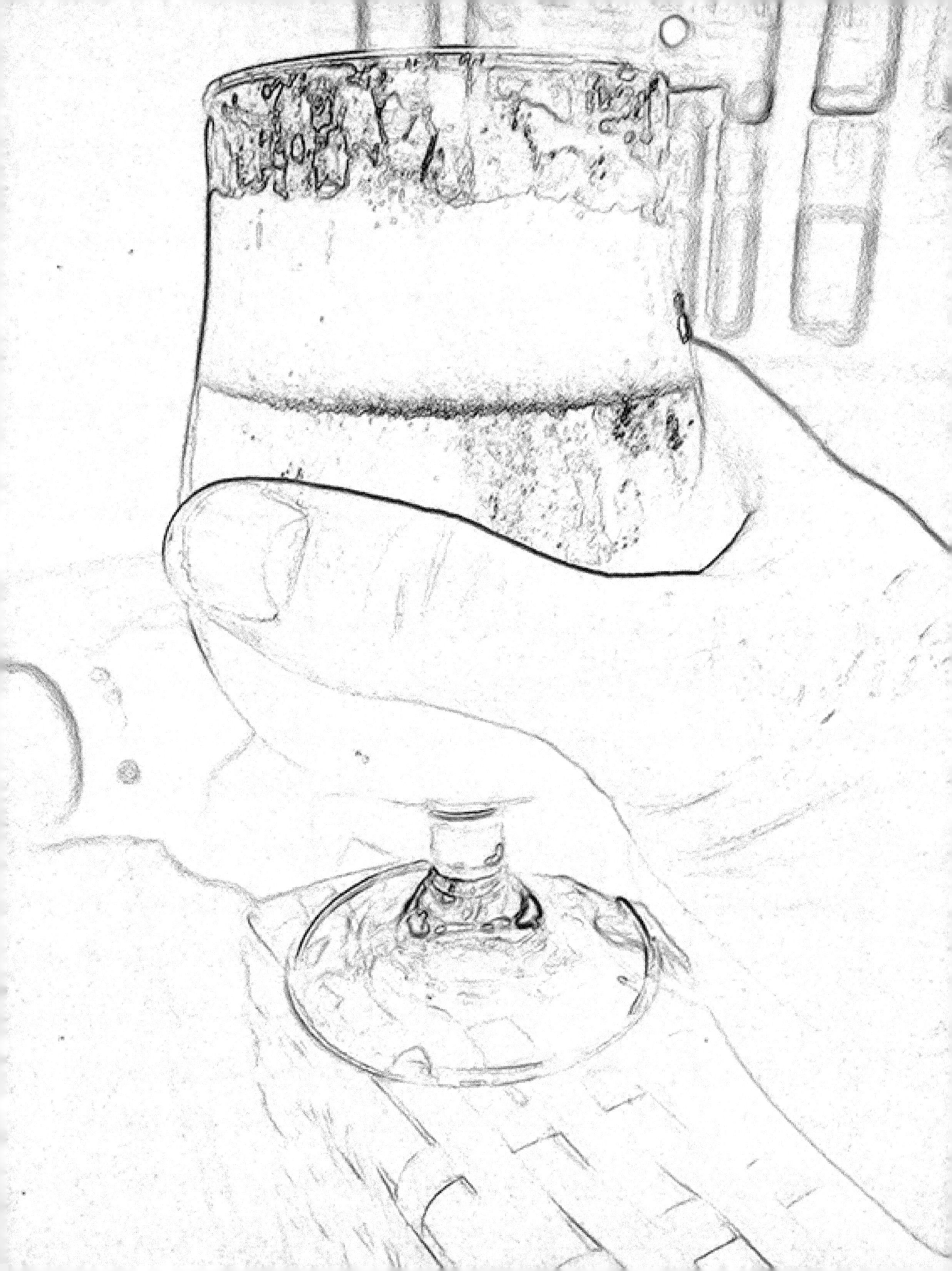

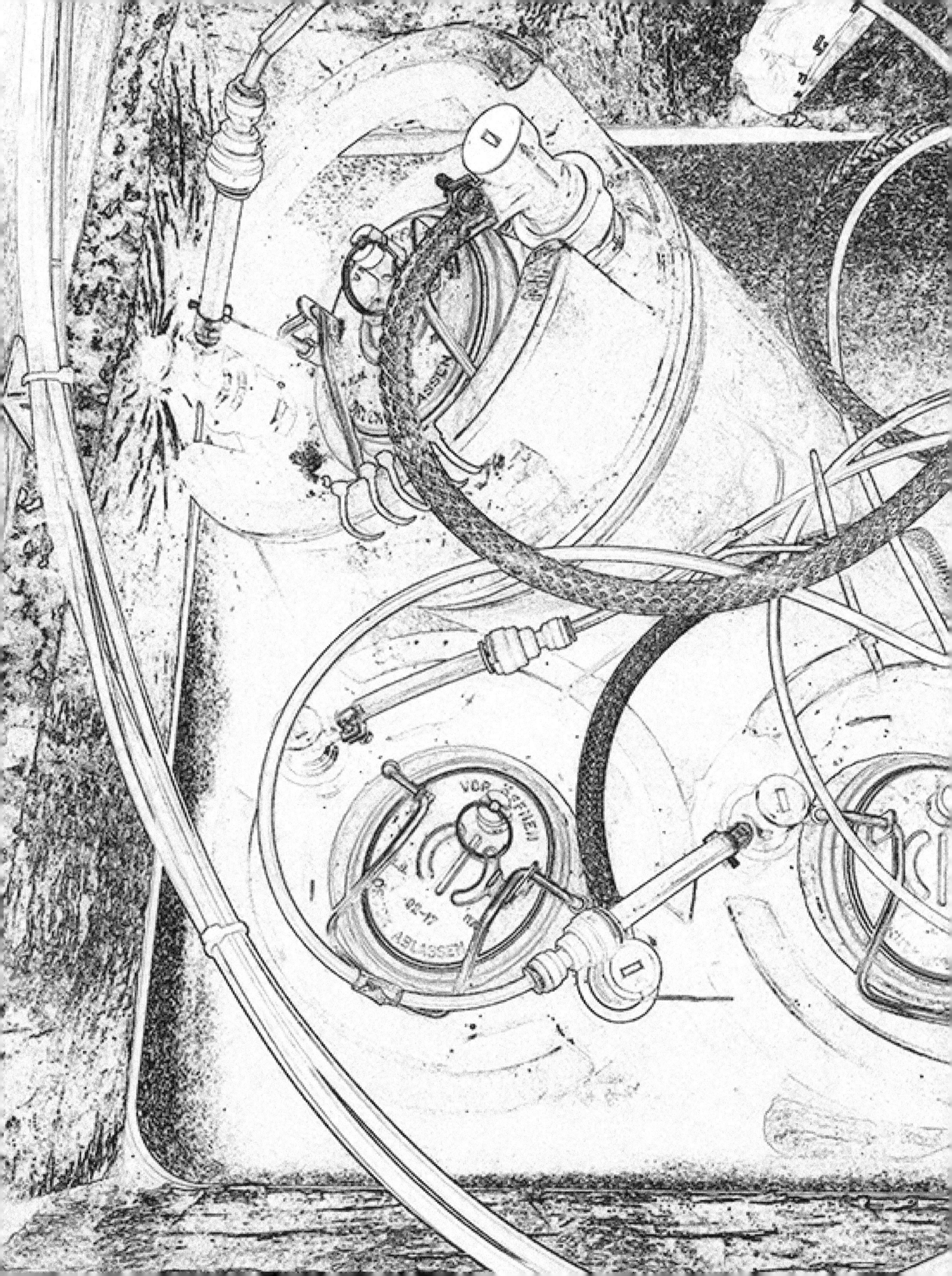

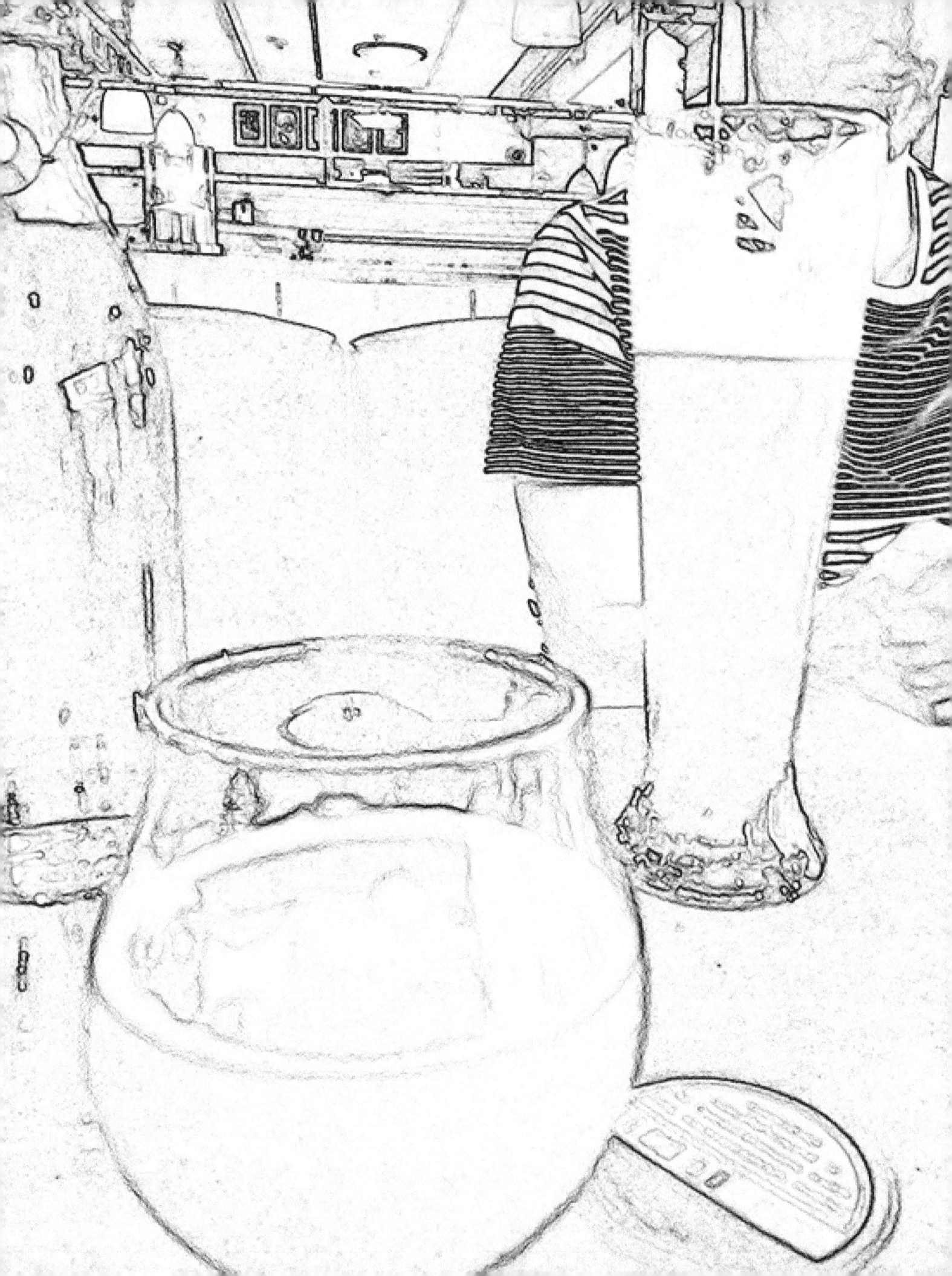

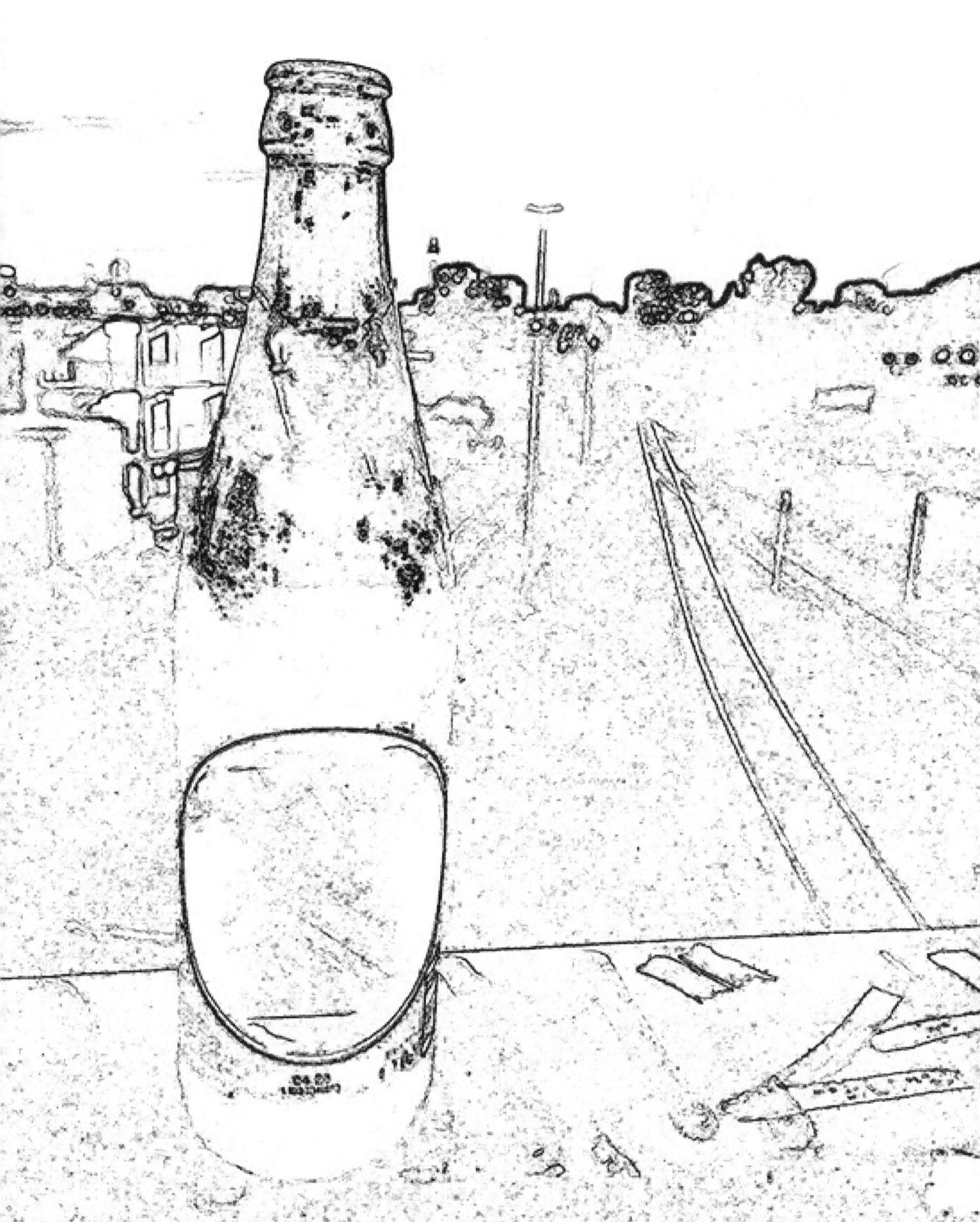

MAKE YOUR OWN BEER CAN

MAKE YOUR OWN BEER CAN

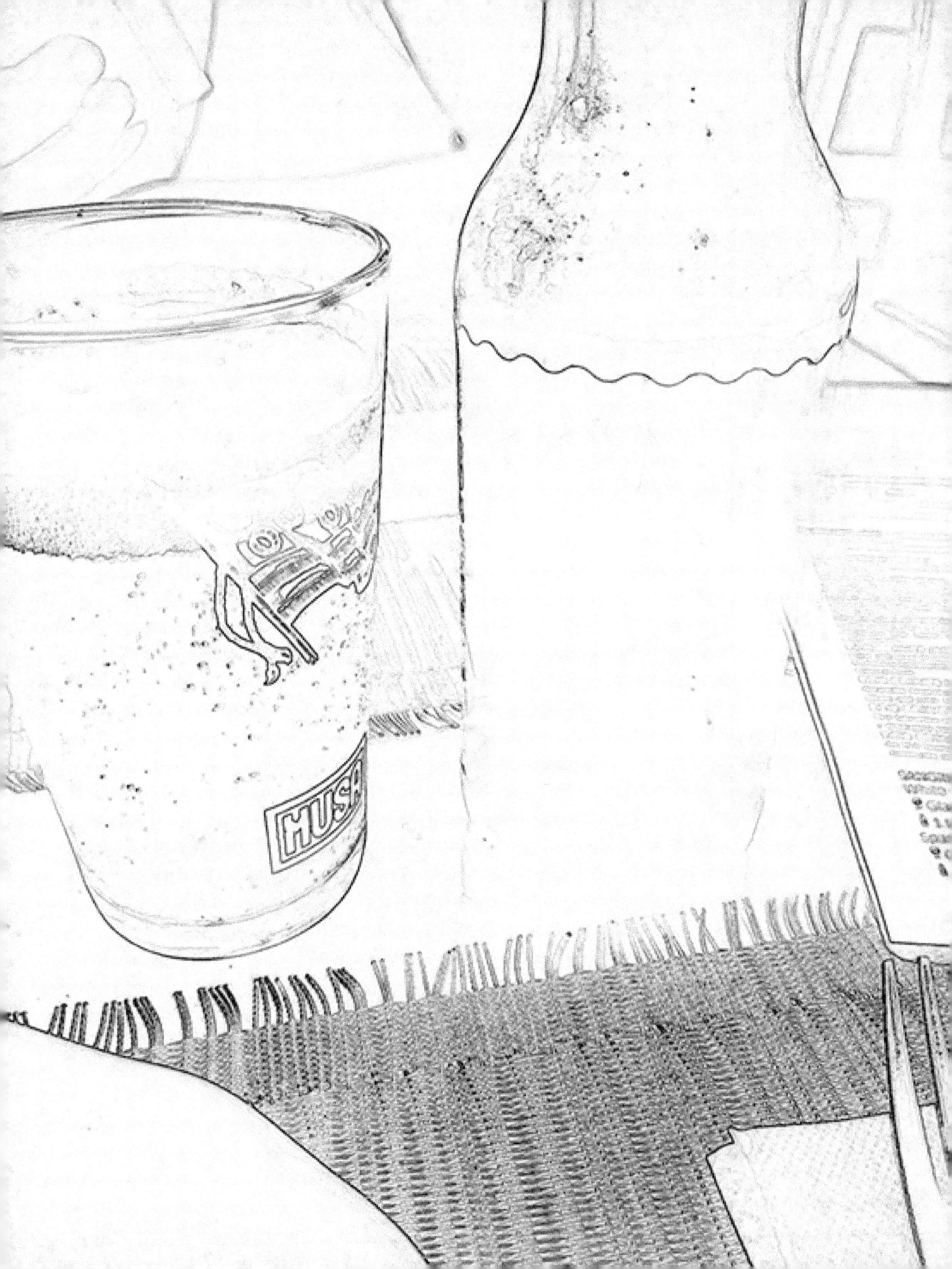

MAKE YOUR OWN BEER BOTTLE

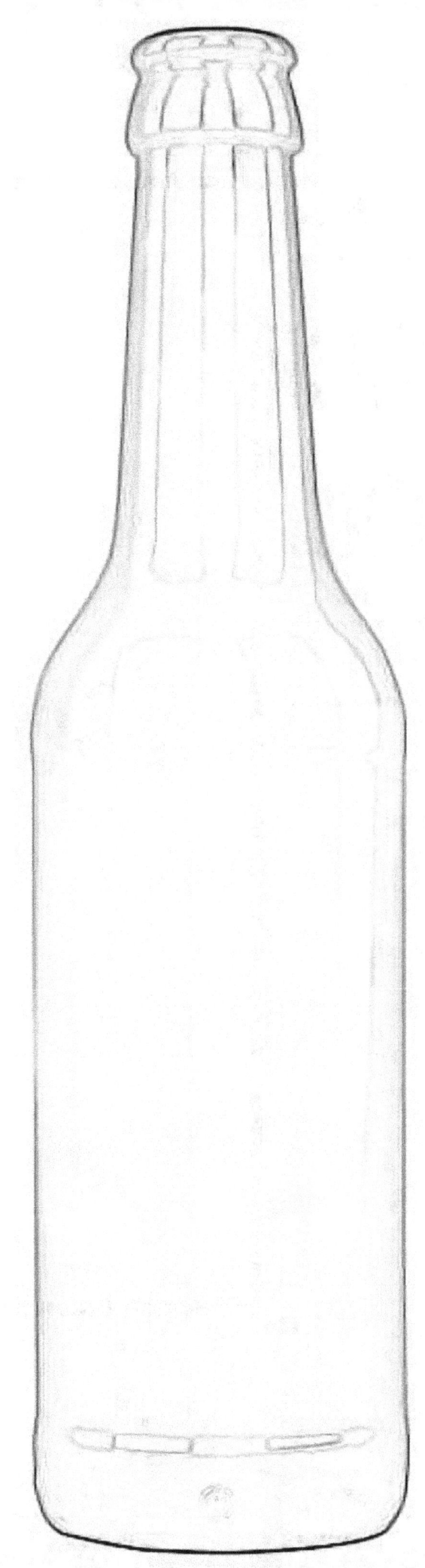

MAKE YOUR OWN BEER LABEL

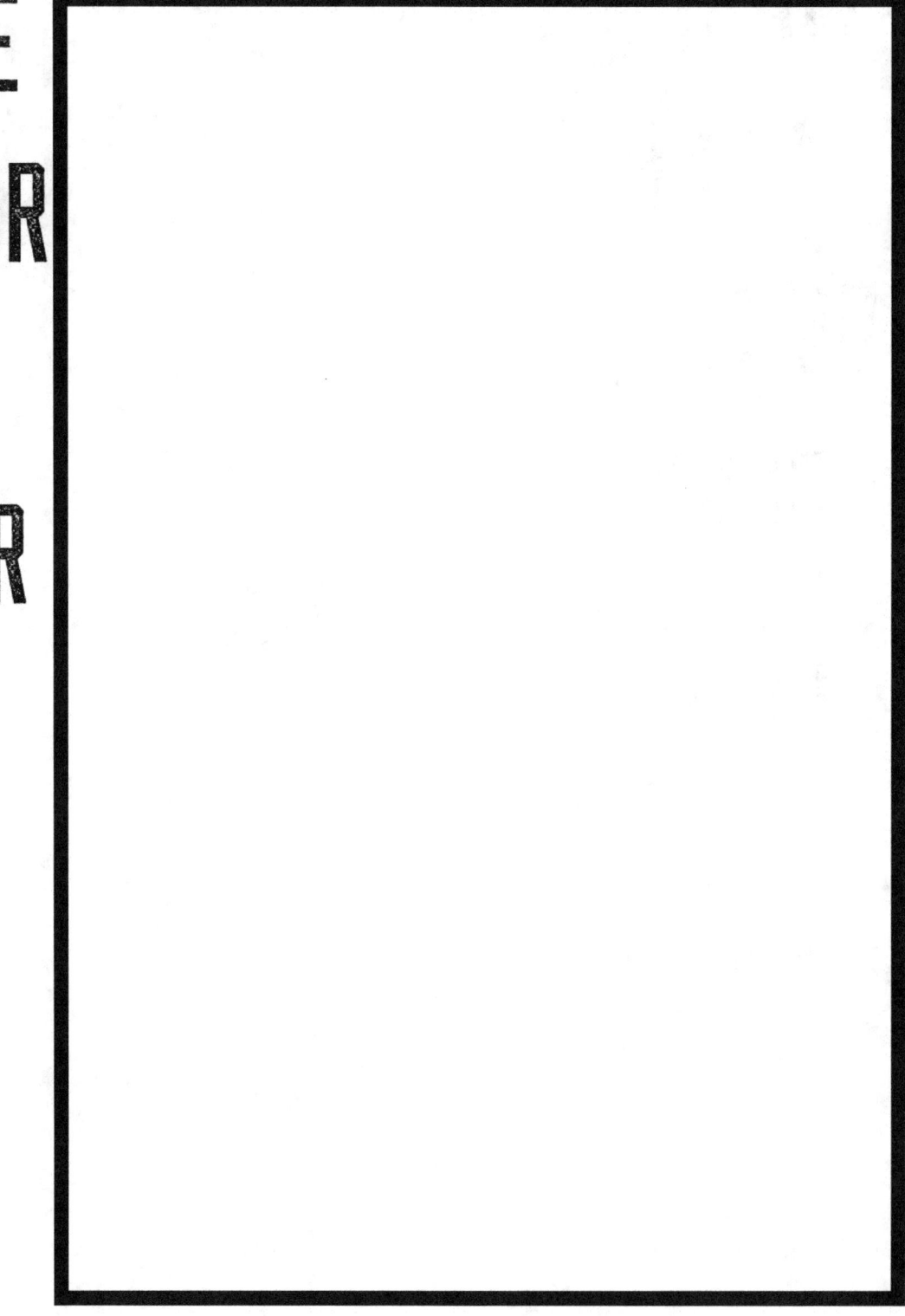

www.ingramcontent.com/pod-product-compliance
Lightning Source LLC
Chambersburg PA
CBHW081701220526
45466CB00009B/2851